THE PROVOCATIVE
BARBARIAN

SAMUEL W. GEISSINGER, JR.

authorHOUSE®

AuthorHouse™
1663 Liberty Drive
Bloomington, IN 47403
www.authorhouse.com
Phone: 1 (800) 839-8640

Published by AuthorHouse 04/11/2019

ISBN: 978-1-7283-0600-1 (sc)
ISBN: 978-1-7283-0602-5 (hc)
ISBN: 978-1-7283-0601-8 (e)

Library of Congress Control Number: 2019903685

Print information available on the last page.

This book is printed on acid-free paper.

DEDICATION

To my daughters, Mother, Father, brother, sisters, Nina M. Day, my best friend, the good people of The Church of St. Richard, without whose prayers this book could not have been written.

Samuel W. Geissinger, Jr.

DISCLAIMER

This book is a fictitious account of described events and experiences of the author. Any likeness to persons now living or deceased is purely coincidental. Names have been changed to protect their privacy.

Samuel W. Geissinger, Jr.

INTRODUCTION

S ome will question what kind of man would volunteer during war time to enter into The United States Air Force in a law enforcement field and remain until retirement at age thirty- seven, help form a **new** United States Air Force while in conflict with North Korea, Vietnam, and The Bay of Pigs.

Some will say that it's barbaric even to temporarily adopt the characteristic of barbarism working undercover as a United States Deputy Sky Marshal, flying all over the world on Transworld Airlines, (TWA), owned by Howard Hughes, to protect our largest commercial (747) aircraft with three hundred fifty passengers and crew aboard, from air piracy. We visited a different country every twenty four hours.

They would also say the same for assuming a similar role as an undercover narcotics agent in The Bureau of Narcotics, Pennsylvania, Office of Attorney General, retiring again at age sixty five with twenty five years of duty.

The barbarian role was assumed so often that sometimes it was difficult to put it down. There were "critters", (that's not nice), people that I had to work with, "rats", (that's not nice), and "animals", (that's not nice either) that had to be arrested because they were very dangerous to our society. Sometimes my role was so important I got arrested right along with everyone else during a big drug raid, just to protect the identity of the "Barbarian".

I have to own the name of the "Barbarian", that's obvious, but you'll have to read on if you're interested in a career that I've described, to find out why it's also "Provocative".

Born and raised in the small town with a big heart, Tamaqua, Pennsylvania.

Samuel W. Geissinger, Jr.

CONTENTS

FOREWORD

Looking back on it today, it all seems like a dream. Like everything else with their quiet beginnings, we can only guess as life progresses, what is in store for us, altering destiny or shaping our lives. Like clockwork either in the direction of the ordinary or the extraordinary. A life of excitement that only a few selected individuals experience, what is it in our past?

The same events which angle one individual in one direction or push another in the opposite direction, this is one of life's great mysteries, one that assures me that **GOD** exists and it's proof that we serve his purpose in some small measure either in an ordinary or extraordinary way. My writings, going back, recalling the events as I've known them may be or may not be the answer, but it is something I must do in closing on a good life.

It began with birth in a small hospital and life in Tamaqua, a small coal mining and railroad town with a rich history of early settlers and the notorious Molly Maguires. This town (Tamaqua) is located in a beautiful valley completely surrounded by mountains in Pennsylvania.

As soon as I outgrew a cradle, I was dropped in bed with my brother who quickly became my mentor. We shared that bed until he went into the Army after graduating from high school. I inherited everything that was my brother's, fishing poles, roller skates, skis, bicycle, his picture of Buck Jones (cowboy) and horse, Silver that was on our dresser from birth, etc. My sisters also shared a room and a bed. Our family was very close. Lovingly my sisters took me to the New York City World's Fair, horse-back riding, etc.

My brother, working in California, took a trip to Tijuana, Mexico and he purchased the most beautiful cowboy outfit for me. It included real cowboy boots, hat, leather cuffs, silk shirt and neck scarf, a hand tooled belt and holster, a beautiful cap gun with pearl handles and spurs for my boots. I was the envy of every child in town.

CHAPTER 1

Tamaqua, Pennsylvania

Tamaqua is an Indian name meaning "Land of Running Water," a quaint, comfortable little town with the Little Schuylkill River running from north to south through it in a valley completely surrounded by beautiful mountains that protect its residents so completely from bad weather or anything else. To travel outside the aforesaid valley in Schuylkill County, either by water (the Little Schuylkill River) or by roads identified by PA Route 209 East or West and Route 309 North or South, it would be necessary to wind your way around mountains. As a child, I did not find many reasons to leave town. Tamaqua is blessed with more water than it can use at a time when surrounding communities are running out of water. Its many reservoirs are helpful to other towns as well. Tamaqua bustled because it also had an overabundance of anthracite coal. Coal was king back then. Environmentalism killed coal and the railroad business which Tamaqua thrived on. It's the only town in the country that has the name "Tamaqua."

The famous Molly Maguires were made up mostly of Irish immigrants whose passage to this country was paid for by mine owners who made indentured servants out of them to mine their coal. While the owners got rich, their servants got badly treated and they rebelled, resorting to murder in many cases. This area is rich with the history of the Molly Maguires.

In Tamaqua lived a man named Baily, one of the two medical doctors in town. Dr. Baily delivered half of the town's residents, including my father in 1903, a sister in 1922, a brother in 1923, a sister in 1925, all planned births, and me (not planned), on New Year's Eve. Everyone was born at home, but I was destined to be born in a hospital, which was state owned and operated in nearby Coaldale, Pennsylvania.

On December 31, 1932, old Doc Baily left a New Year's Eve party to deliver me. When my Father inquired as to the doc's fee, he replied, "Happy New Year. Just give me one of those fat chickens you're raising down at the Train Station where you work." He referred to chickens that were rescued from broken crates in the Railway Express cars. Those chickens seemed to grow much bigger than other similar chickens. They were an oddity to all who knew of them. When I was in first grade, I developed whooping cough. Mother took me to Doc Baily. He treated me and told Mother to take me home and put me in bed. Mother did as instructed but learned that I had difficulty breathing. Mother contacted Doc Baily, who arrived with an injection for diphtheria, which he said developed from whooping cough. After chasing me all over the bedroom, my mother and Dr. Baily got that injection in me, which they said saved my life.

My grandfather worked as a car Inspector for the railroad with tracks that passed so close to his home on Hazle Street in Tamaqua, he could step off the bank behind his house on to the train whose cars he inspected, spend the day on the train, and get home the same way.

My father quit school at age fifteen to earn money to help support his family. He worked at the bottom of a coal mine at first. It was as low as you could get. It was called "mucking" or picking slate, which was a hard, risky, and unhealthy job for young boys. He left and went to work driving a

horse and buggy delivering ice in summer and coal in winter. He was raised in a family of four boys and five girls in a small town where his ancestors had lived for many generations. He was a big man blessed with big hands made strong by competing with his brothers as a child and hard work at the bottom of mines at fifteen and loading and unloading a wagon with coal using only a number ten scoop (a shovel) and loading huge cakes of ice on a leather-covered shoulder at age sixteen.

At seventeen years of age, Grandpop got my dad a job driving a horse and buggy for the Railway Express Company. On the first day they handed him the reins of a big black gelding and told him to get him ready for work delivering express in Tamaqua. Dad walked his new horse up the track where Hagerty's blacksmith was to get him shod. The farrier asked Dad the name of his horse. When Dad replied that he did not have a name, the farrier suggested Dad could name his horse Doug, after the famous movie star Douglas Fairbanks. Doug kept that name until he was replaced by a Railway Express truck. I used to love riding alongside my dad when he delivered express packages in town. I can still hear the sound that the horse's hooves made crossing the old covered wooden bridges, one on the south side and one on the north side of town. Dad told a story about Doug: when Dad got sick, he got called out of his sick bed because Doug would not move for the substitute driver. Dad figured it out right away. He stopped outside a store where Dad made daily deliveries, and Dad always grabbed a cracker from a barrel in that store for Doug, something that the substitute driver didn't know.

In winter, some of the hills old Doug had to pull a heavy wagon up were steep and sometimes frozen. He would have to struggle and I felt so bad for him when he slipped and went down on his knees. Dad would get off immediately and render first aid to Doug's scraped knees.

My great-grandfather on my father's side owned and ran his own business on Hunter Street in Tamaqua. He was a shoemaker (1827–1909).

My dad became very popular. Well-known people often spoke of his great strength when he was seen loading and unloading large items from his wagon as a daily routine.

Tamaqua was a great place to grow up. I learned to love horses and animals in general. I could not own a pony or horse because of limited space, but there were riding stables where I rented ponies or horses. I owned a dog from day one. Wherever I went, my dog went with me.

I had many friends with whom I shared everything. We knew everyone in town. I always felt safe and there was very little crime.

Mother's family originated from the Allentown area. Mother's family came to Tamaqua when her father was hired to manage a sewing machine factory where every one of his daughters was employed when they reached the age of fifteen. This included my mother until she met and married my father in Tamaqua.

Now to Tamaqua's attraction: the Bungalow. We had a nice swimming pool and bathhouse, a stand to buy food as needed, a picnic area with cover as needed, and water and fireplaces for cooking. We could never wait until the official pool opened. We didn't have to.

The river and surrounding mountains afforded us children with many amusements, some of which were quite mysterious. We named them all. The Red Bridge was a railroad crossing the Little Schuylkill River, approximately three miles North of Tamaqua. It was popular because we tied a rope to the bridge over the river and could swing from a big rock and jump off into a deep hole. This is where I learned to swim after coming close to drowning a couple of times. Another favorite hole for swimming was named The Saddle because of the big rock in the middle, shaped like a saddle and great for sunbathing. There were two wires, one up, one down, strung across the river close to the highway and the power lines. These were there for the power line inspectors to cross the water without getting wet. We boys used to race to these wires because whoever made it across first avoided getting wet. The first one across would shake the bottom wire vigorously in order to make the others fall in the river. There was a waterfall nearby, covered with moss, making it slippery for sliding off on our bare butts while our clothes dried. Did I say it was close to the highway? Yes, we got a lot of horn blowing.

Then there was Paradise, my favorite destination, a high cliff on one side with two trees side by side worn as a crown at the very top. On the opposite side there was a soft, sandy beach. Depending on the size of our group, you could be amused all day just watching friends climbing the cliff and jumping or diving in the river, always ready to assist in case of an accident. The object of our intentions was, depending on your courage, to dive or jump from between the two trees at the very top. There was always a lot of tension when we realized someone in our group was going for it. What was nice was that it was so secluded—good for nude swimming.

Our surrounding mountains may not be the highest, but to a child who labored up to the top of one, when we made it, we were soaring. Being able to look down on our little town below us was so invigorating. At the very top of one of our mountains was a very big flat rock townspeople named "Table Rock". We children named others, "Tarzan's Cave", which we used as a hiding place in games we played. Another formation of large boulders we named "Elephant Rock". Another, just known as the "High Bridge", a railway bridge so high it made you dizzy and some refused to cross because you might interrupt the travel of a train mid-way across. When we boys felt a little more adventurous, we'd climb to the top of the High Bridge from the river bottom. The trails on either side of the bridge

that led to the bottom were very steep and you had to be careful that your momentum did not move you too fast because you would likely be smeared all over the ground at the bottom. One day while walking carefully down one of those trails, I was about to step on a sun bathing snake. Jumping over the snake got me moving too fast. It was all I could do to keep my legs under me. I managed to make it to the bottom but it was inevitable I suffered many bruised, cuts, scrapes, etc. from my fall among the rocks, bushes, etc. We learn quickly in circumstances like these, the hard way. Tamaqua was a giant amusement park to us. A few miles North of Tamaqua was Hometown. A few miles West of Hometown was Barnesville where Lakeside and Lakewood Amusement Parks were located.

I, along with friends with girlfriends, would like to gather for a trip to Barnesville to enjoy the day at the amusement parks. Mother explained that she could not give me the money but if I made a bag of coal, she would be able to pay me for the coal delivered to her (our coal bin). I would crack coal, bag it and haul it home on my wagon from the closest mountain until I had enough money for the day's outing. This is why I thank my Mother every day. She developed a work ethic in me which survives until this day. I worked and payed in to Social Security every Summer, either as an electrician's helper or on a farm from the surrounding area. I worked as a bellhop in Tamaqua's Majestic Hotel and I helped people from the railroad direct traffic with gates and lights and weights. Anything I wanted I had to work for. One of my prized possessions until this day was a pump action Remington. A scope was added much later, a .22 caliber rifle. As many of my friends lucky enough to own a rifle gathered every weekend for our adventures along the river or the mountains and woods, devising targets to shoot at that floated, like an empty match box, which sank when hit. We got good!

I was so proud of my Father. My hero was admired by many of the town's people. Dad volunteered as a firefighter at the Citizens Fire Company in Tamaqua. He was a charter member. It made me proud to hear of his exploits in that regard. During parades throughout the state, he looked handsome in his dress uniform, riding or driving on one of the fire company's fire engines.

Dad decided to try his hand at politics. He campaigned for the town council in the middle ward of Tamaqua and he was elected. This position required him to have a private line telephone when most others could only have a party line. Dad bought his first automobile at a time when few automobiles were in existence. If I remember correctly, it was a Terroplane. Both movie picture theaters and restaurants in Tamaqua provided our family with discounts in their facilities.

Dad was promoted from one of the many drivers to the head position of the Railway Express Agency at the Tamaqua Train Station. Many nights were spent by my Dad perfecting his penmanship and improving his math skills to prepare for his newly elected/promoted positions.

Dad served the community in many ways. For example, because Tamaqua had limited big store capabilities he would handle a citizen's money and request, for say, a child's bicycle. The money which he put on the train to Philadelphia, or some other big city and delivered the child's bicycle upon the return trip.

1937 TAMAQUA RAILWAY EXPRESS AGENT &
TOWN COUNCELMAN ~ MIDDLEWARD

He attended all of the town council meetings and, as a charter member, he served on the Citizens Fire Company Board by helping it to stay ready to respond on a moment's notice.

Dad's popularity, as it does in so many cases, led to his downfall, his indiscrimination. There was a woman and a child involved and our family asked him to leave our home.

As an Express Agent in charge, he handled a lot of money. He had to move to Mahanoy City with his new pregnant woman. He had to resign as Councilman in Tamaqua. He had seniority with the railroad so he bumped the Express Agent in Mahanoy City. When the Railroad Company learned of his new lifestyle, they took away his seniority, demoting him to the position as Messenger, meaning he would ride inside a railcar delivering freight to each station where the train stopped.

My Mother, a small woman in stature, dignified, well kept, slender, kindly and beautiful, I don't ever remember seeing her in any shoes other than high heels, she was loyal to her own family and was loved so much by her own children. Other men wanted her but being the only child remaining with her in our home, I can honestly say that she never looked to another man except for my Father. Mother would never agree to divorce Father, which was required to get divorced then. She knew he would return to us eventually.

I was eight when he left and I used to get on the train in Tamaqua, show up at his office in Mahanoy City when I missed him so much. Father would call my Mother so she would not worry. I made many attempts to persuade my Father to show him how important it was to have him in our lives. At last he could not be persuaded. He had lost so much.

My youngest sister married a young man who was drafted into the Army. He had a problem with alcohol and difficulty with the law. He spent a lot of time in an Army Brig and never advanced in rank.

My Mother had difficulty with expenses and invited my sister to share expenses. Her husband beat my sister and I and threatened to beat my Mother. He would come home drunk and because I stood up for my family, he beat me and he was cruel to my dog. As his adult hands lashed out at my child's (ten years old) face and body, I would ask myself would he dare do this to me if Dad or my Brother were here. Questions many children ask of themselves when there are no Father figures in their lives. I vowed then that I would always be in my children's lives and I've done that. Where was he?

Why my Mother never left me down and why she had such a good influence in my life is exemplified by what she did next. She had her whole family whom she was so close to in Tamaqua, but she did the only thing she could do to protect us from the cruelty of my brother-in-law.

As an example of how bad he was (brother-in law), he brought a Japanese gun home from the Pacific. He carried it around in his belt. One night a friend and I came home after spending time with our girlfriends. As we approached my house I said to my friend that I must go to the rear of my house and get our garbage out to be picked up the next day, As I entered the alley, I tripped on something I was not familiar with. When I put my foot down, it moved and moaned. My Mother came to the front door, unlocked it to let me enter, then locked it again. My Mother explained that my drunken brother-in-law had his gun and was sleeping it off in the alley way. I must have awakened him because he started making a commotion in the neighborhood. Shots were fired some said at a neighbor complaining about the commotion. Cops came, took his gun and put him in jail.

Sometimes I learned to avoid a beating by running to the upstairs bathroom, locking the door and escaping by jumping out the window onto a porch roof next door, then jumping to the ground. Sometimes I'd hide for days before I thought it was safe enough to go home. I kept asking myself would my brother-in-law dare beat us if my Farther or even my brother were there?

Santa Monica, California

My big brother, a long time weight lifter, after high school graduation and more than three years in the Army, European Theater, attained the rank of Corporal, was honorably discharged. He found work with an Army friend from Tamaqua in Santa Monica, California as a skilled machinist, working for Douglas Aircraft. He lived in his friend's wife's home where he rented a room. Mother wrote to him and he sent money for Mother and I to travel by bus to his home. When we got there we learned he had purchased a house trailer and rented space in the rear yard of those same friends for the three of us to live. Mother was employed making beds and cleaning rooms in a hotel. I was enrolled as a new student in John Adams Junior High School, where they promoted every half year. It was customary to enroll new students one half year behind the year you had advanced to when you arrived. This meant that I was now a half year behind all my classmates I schooled with all my life in Tamaquq.

At times my brother would ask me to help him by climbing onto the trailer roof to remove avocados that dropped onto the roof from the tree above it. If allowed to rot on the roof, the roof would rot and leak. Another time he and I worked on a 1933 Plymouth, restoring the engine. As a reward

my brother took my Mother and I to California's Yosemite State Park to see the giant Redwoods up close, drive through them and see people who carved them out to live in them, learn the Indian legends about fire falls, see it fall, see half dome mountains, etc. This was something I never forgot, my brother also took my Mother and I to the annual New Year's Day Parade in Pasadena, California. We slept on the curb the night before my birthday so we would have a good place to see the parade. Another memorable moment I could never forget.

In California at John Adams Junior High School, as a young man, I had to earn my position among all the other students who at fifteen, could own cars, be licensed and drive. Many children had souped-up vehicles all chopped up which they raced. I couldn't and didn't want to fit in. One day in particular, my brother gave me a dime to buy a treat from the school cafeteria. He knew Mother packed sandwiches for me every day to save money. Eager to purchase that treat, I was running to make my purchase. I dropped my dime and it rolled in the direction of a person I knew to be a gang member. He put his foot on my dime. I asked him to remove his foot from my dime. He showed me a picture from his wallet of Joe Lewis, a World Champion Boxing Champion, who he claimed was his brother and he assured me I would get my ass kicked. He denied any knowledge of my dimes location. I pushed him, recovered my dime, waited to see what he might do. He wasn't sure about me because I was new at his school. He decided not to do anything and life was better for me at that school after that. Getting beatings from my brother-in-law, a full sized adult gave me enough courage to stand my ground with another child. I had no fear of them.

My brother could only afford a second-hand bicycle which I was mighty grateful for. I began to wonder how I could use the bike to earn money to help out. I would travel daily to the Santa Monica Pier where I learned to get bait to fish with. Mussels extracted from the piers pillings were easy to get. As a matter of fact, they used to wash up on the beach south of Santa Monica Pier and that beach was named Mussel Beach. Many body builders displayed their abilities, freely taking advantage of the beach's name. Many people would arrive daily and take in the free show. I myself sat and watched. I sat next to Dorothy Lamour, "Sarong Girl" in Bob Hope, Bing Crosby Road Movies.

The best bait I could get was from friends I made at a cannery located on the pier. I would take parts of fish which were discarded. They used to discard lobster legs, the small ones, there wasn't much meat in them. They were cooked and I used to fill my shirt with them. Then I would go to the end of the pier, throw my pole in the water and fish while eating the lobster legs. I'd break them off at each end and suck the meat out, just like eating peanuts. Small fish used to gather below where I was sitting and I learned how to snag them on a line, full of hooks. I used to clean these small fish on the pier and I learned how to tie a piece of fish on to a small net to attract crabs. Our family sure enjoyed eating them fresh out of the water. While fishing and eating just off the end of the pier, I would bait up my big pole and throw it out as far I could. I began catching small sharks about four or five feet long. Sharks were no good to me so I would just cut them up and throw them back in the water.

I saw a man watching me discard the shark. He approached and told me he was a doctor who would pay me fifteen dollars a pound for shark liver which he needed to make vitamins. That man made a shark fisherman out of me. We tired quickly of the few fish I brought hone for the table, but we never tired of the doc's money for shark liver.

It hardly ever rained. There is a lot of wind off of that ocean which made it comfortable night or day, I rode my bike every day after school on holidays and weekends in almost two years there. I lived my life like that. I had a friend that shared his surfboard with me and we rescued a baby seal with it for days we observed the baby crying for his mother who never returned, he stayed on the break water until we paddled out, put him on the surfboard and paddled him back to the pier.

There was a diving attraction. People, tourists mostly, paid to be lowered in a fake water diving bell to observe the creatures under water. When the owner saw us with the baby seal, he said he'd be happy to make him the added attraction and care for him on the pier. We could go see him any time we wanted to! We were happy with that arrangement, said so and said goodbye.

Mother and I missed Tamaqua, it started to grow on us, so we began to make plans for our return.

There was an old dog at the pier that welcomed me each time I appeared. He looked for me and the food we shared. He was obviously a bum. I couldn't take him home because there was no room so he stayed at the pier and I at home. I would feel bad when I had to go home. That old dog was the final nail. We were ready to go back to Tamaqua.

Money, packing, bus, one week travel, "Tamaqua", here we come. Mother greeting family, me greeting all my friends in a grade above me now. Very happy meeting an old girlfriend, someone I didn't find time to do much thinking about. Now I'm looking and thinking too much about. High school is too early to become sexually active. Many of my friends were sexually active in junior high school.

My friends who will graduate a year ahead of me are talking about going into the Navy. I wanted to go with them. I had a discussion with my parents. Yes, I said parents. Surely you guessed it. My Dad's girlfriend left him for a guy in the Air Force. Without the big money, the important job, no divorce, gone all the time, what else was she to do? He called home when he heard we were home. He asked me if I thought Mother would take him back. I told him we knew he would be back, that we loved him. Dad asked me if I would meet him at the Train Station and walk home with him for support. I met him, we walked home together and he was home. He had learned a lesson and never strayed again. "**MY HERO HAD RETURNED**"!

History of Lehigh County, Volume 2, Pages 369 and 370
Mother's Fogel Family Ancestry

Philip Gabriel von Vogel, a native of Hanan Chur Hesse, Germany, emigrated to America upon the ship "Samuel" which landed at Philadelphia August 17, 1731. He was a son of Philip Carl August von Vogel, a Dragon of the Royal Prussian Cavalry and he died in 1791. To them the patent of nobility was granted on October 2, 1786. Upon arrival of the American ancestor, he located in Bucks County, Pennsylvania. In 1734 he moved to Lynn Township, now Lehigh County where he owned more than 500 acres of land situated along the North side of the Schochary Hills, near New Tripoli, Pennsylvania. The homestead property is now owned by Jacob Mosser. There the pioneer ancestor of the von Vogel family is buried in a private burial ground situated about 125 feet due South from the present brick house occupied by Mr. Mosser.

Upon settling in Lynn Township, Philip Gabriel von Vogel erected a most substantial log house which served as a fort and place of refuge for himself and the settlers of the surrounding locality against the attack of savage Indians between the years of 1755 and 1763. (See History of Vogel House in Lynn Township.) The house also was the nucleus of the reformed branch of the Ebenezer Church at New Tripoli. In it the first store was kept in the township, which business was continued for more than a century.

The pioneer was the Father of five children: Viz, Conrad, Johann, Jacob, Mrs. Weber, whose descendants still reside in the same locality, and a Mrs. Smith.

John Vogel, son of Conrad, the oldest son of Philip Gabriel, was born September 15, 1753 in Lynn Township. He moved to Upper Macungie Township near Fogelsville and died April 25, 1816.

Solomon Fogel moved close to Breinigsville. His wife was Maria Breinig, daughter of Colonel George Breinig of Revolutionary fame.

Tilghman Street in Allentown, Pennsylvania was named after a well-known blind musician, Amandus Fogel's son, Tilghman Fogel, born on August 11, 1842 and died October 10, 1915.

These records are the earliest records found of my pioneer ancestors. It all began with the arrival in Philadelphia, Pennsylvania of Philip Gabriel von Vogel on the good ship Samuel August 17, 1731. Pioneers who settled in this country founding fathers of whom I'm very proud. If I've been in love with my country and served it well, it's because that's what I've been bred to do.

CHAPTER 2

The United States Air Force

My parents knew how upset I was being left behind by my best friends and being in a grade behind those that I attended school with all of my life. I promised that I would do what I had to do to improve my educational standards once I was in service. Now that I quit school, my friends who had already graduated from high school, decided not to join the Navy. I joined my first choice which had always been the United States Air Force, the best decision I ever made. Those same friends later married and joined the United States Navy. Four years later they were discharged and complained that they were separated from their wives, on a ship, sea sick all the time and they had enough of the Navy.

On April 8, 1951, the day before Dad's birthday, the Air Force flew me and approximately six other acquaintances from Tamaqua to Lackland Air Force Base in San Antonio, Texas for basic training. Strengthen our faith, increase our love for one another, and send us forth into the world in courage and peace, rejoicing in the power of the Holy Spirit; through Jesus Christ our Savior. Amen.

Pictures on the news channels on the TV at that time were of Americans with hands tied behind their backs, shot in the back of their heads and thrown in a roadside ditch.

THE FIRST PICTURE TAKEN

The first commercially successful computer was completed in 1951. Improvements like programming, microchips, software, and memory banks followed one another. Besides its military use in ballistics, the computer made space exploration possible. Its speed enabled ground controllers to put rockets and satellites into orbit and chart their precise course. It enabled astronauts to build space stations where scientists could remain for months at a time. A new U.S. Air Force (four years old), was a perfect place and time for a young man like me to get out there and start making history, a time to make a young life exciting, good or bad. Coal mining and railroads in Tamaqua were dying, killed by environmentalism. The entire region was economically depressed.

We were at cold war with North Korea. Patriotic men from all walks of life rushed to join the fight. The basic training camps were all over-crowded. We slept on cots in tents, polished our boots under street lights, sitting on a curb. Worst of all we stood in line to use toilets and bathing facilities in the barracks. If you took more than ten minutes in the bathing facilities, you had to leave or get back in line again. We did half of our basic training there then they shipped us up to Sheppard Air Force Base in Wichita, Texas where we lived in barracks and we finished our basic training.

Things have really changed since those days. Today (2016) it sickens me to see how the National Anthem was a song that made men and women stand together and fight to keep this country free. Now a few individuals refusing to stand for the singing of the National Anthem is growing and separating us more every day. I just witnessed a singer of our National Anthem kneeling while singing our National Anthem on TV.

It seems to me that our last Memorial Day (2016) was changed from remembering **ALL** members of the military, black or white, who died defending our country and keeping it safe, "to let us not forget that white people kept slaves." The TV gave us a whole week of the movie ROOTS. All white people need is their conscience to remind them of that, the same conscience that provides us with all the civil rights laws that over-compensate blacks in fairness to them.

President Harry Truman did not seek re-election. The election of Dwight D. Eisenhower as President in 1952 helped to allay Americans nerves. The Generals stature as Supreme Commander of Allied Forces in Europe inspired confidence and trust, especially among the military.

Richard Milhous Nixon, another ex-military Congressman and Senator, was his running mate.

In 2016, the most effective watchdog group, Judicial Watch, has stated that the fact is that corruption in American Government is a very serious problem. During Barack Obama's Presidency especially, we've witnessed an explosion of scandals, abuses of power, all serious violations of public trust. The Obama Administration has shown contempt for the separation of power and the U. S. Constitution, exploded the size and reach of our Government, corruptly nationalized our health care industry, granted unlawful back door amnesty for millions of illegal aliens and attacked many of our freedoms across the board. Barack Obama, Hillary Clinton, and their appointees have failed the integrity test completely so when we look at the ethical misbehavior of elected officials and government bureaucrats today. One would think that our societies morals and values have shifted and tragically not for the better.

In 1951 I applied for Radar Maintenance training thinking that might be something I could use when I left the service. Instead they sent me to Biloxi Air Force Base in Mississippi for training in the Radar Operation field. I found the training to be interesting and I was looking forward to putting my training to good use. When I was notified that I was to be retrained as a Military Policeman, the Radar Operation field was overcrowded and it would serve as a secondary field of training for me if needed in the future.

I was then shipped to Tyndall Air Force Base, Panama City, Florida, for training in the Military Police career field. This training was much more physical and more suited to my background. It seemed I was training with a class of city slickers who were not very physical and obviously not familiar with firearms. I stood out and was given leadership positions thanks to the good old .22 caliber pump action Remington rifle we tinkered with on our weekly outings with my school chums in Tamaqua.

When I first arrived at Tyndall, I was looking for a room to throw my junk in. I ran into a bunch of guys, good natured, and since the rooms supported eight guys, I decided to throw my gear in their room. I didn't know it at the time, but I soon learned that they were all Italian. They were always joking with each other and they referred to each other as "WOP". I laughed right along with them until one of them called me a "WOP". I understood how they could make that mistake. I looked more Italian than some of them, dark brown hair, dark brown eyes and dark tanned skin. When I told them I was an American Dutchman, they said, "If we had known that, they would not let me in their room." I asked what they would like to do about it. They laughed, hugged me and from that day on I was known as Dutch. I did say they were good natured didn't I? Having finished our police training, we all received our new assignments. I learned that

I was being stationed at Mitchell Air Force Base in Hempstead, New York. The guy I enjoyed being with the most, the one that I had most in common with, we'll call "Vinny". He was from New York and he learned he would be stationed in Louisiana. I was happy with my assignment because I could go home to Tamaqua every weekend if I liked. Vinny was unhappy with his assignment so far away from his home in Portchester, New York. Vinny said he had a "Goomba" (friend), female, whom he promised he would find an airman to write to her. He asked me to do him a favor and write to her. I told him I had a girl in Tamaqua. He said it didn't matter, she'd be happy to hear from me. I agreed and I did write to her. She was a nice girl. We got along well by mail and she asked me to visit her. I took a weekend to visit her in Portchester. She took me to meet her family and Vinny's family. I even met Vinny's girl, the one he was engaged to. They were all so nice and Vinny thanked me for doing so. I dated the girl, (Goomba), a few more times and I ran into my Dad's ex-girlfriend, my half-sister and her Air Force husband. My half-sister didn't know me and her mother rushed her away. I never saw them again. Then I got shipped down to Langley Air Force Base, Virginia, in preparation for shipment to England.

While at Langley Air Force Base, I had a discussion with the girl I was dating in Tamaqua. She was in nurses training at the time. We talked about the possibility of marriage and her accompanying me over to England. She said her Aunt and Uncle were paying for her training and they would be hurt if she quit. On the last night before I had to go back to Langley to be shipped to England, we went roller skating and later it got hot and heavy and we both had clumsy first time sex in the back seat of Dad's car. Before I left Langley Air Force Base, our clumsy first time sex advanced quite quickly. With Dad on the road all week and Mother working every day, we played house. It was a wonderful learning process, running through the house naked, marveling at each new discovery.

When I first arrived at Mitchel Air Force Base, I met this guy I'll call Frank. He was a tall, lanky Southern boy from Tennessee. He was covered in freckles. He was an Air Policeman like me, receiving his training on the job. Frank and I were sent to Langley Air Force Base, Virginia, where we met a man everyone called "Harry the Horse". He was a big man, very forceful with a loud voice and decisive action that made every word sound like a growl. At present he only had a couple of stripes on his sleeve. He didn't need any. Everyone wanted to know Harry. It was immediately understood Harry was a force to be respected and someone who would not take any crap. He got my respect immediately. He reminded me of my Dad. I became an Airman I could relate to the minute I met Harry. The story of Harry as he related it to me when we became friends is as follows: Harry joined the Army way back when the Army relied on horses and mules for transportation and for moving equipment. His first specialty was as a farrier. He was the one who put the shoes on horses and mules, most of them who were rank or untrained. It took a real man to do this work. His farrier experience can be credited with making Harry the big strong man he was when I first met him. Another big man that we all met when we first came to Langley was our new Commander, Colonel Dunning who was given so much responsibility as Commander of the Twentieth Fighter Bomber wing which had never been integrated. He knew that there would be problems especially because we were shipping out to England with very few people of the black race. Harry's history was well known to Colonel Dunning. Harry had been a top sergeant in the past and the rules were completely changed. In the past you corrected them with force against anyone under your command. Harry had a young man in his command who jeopardized everyone's health with his uncleanliness. Harry gave this young man a GI (Government Issued) shower with a GI brush. That's the way it was always done but the rules had changed. Harry was court marshaled and sent to prison and he was to be dishonorably discharged. But as Harry related his story, Walter Winchell (Radio News Broadcaster), of great fame used his influence and Harry's fate was reconsidered allowing him to return to military duty, but he had to start at the bottom and work his way up through the ranks.

Colonel Dunning, Commander, determined Harry was just the man to solve all of his integration problems, leaving him with only the bigger problems of his mission. It was said that Colonel Dunning handed Harry a bed adaptor, a long metal bar normally intended for use in joining one bed on top of another. All he said was, "Integrate them". There were problems, fights, arguments, etc., but they soon stopped after Harry chased us out into the streets, sometimes at two or three in the morning, marching to Harry's deep voiced cadence. Until this day I get an urge to snap to attention when I hear that voice in my dreams.

I knew I would always respect Harry. Harry represented authority, the rules, the law. In my opinion, a swift kick in the ass should be written into the Military Code of Conduct.

Frank and I traveled from Langley Air Force Base, Virginia to Wethersfield Air Force Base, England, together by boat or if I was a Navy man, more correctly, a ship. I knew now why my Navy friends did not like the Navy. Almost every one suffered from sea sickness. When I asked Navy friends about it later, they told me they were sick all the time. They would be sick a while and work a while.

The Air Force was only four years old when I joined. I was issued one brown Army Air Corps and one blue Air Force uniform. We had to dye our boots and make them shine. Our mission was one of great importance to the war effort in Korea. We were taking the atomic weapon overseas for the first time in peace time, (highly classified). Even the shape of it was classified. The assigned aircraft jet propelled F-84 fighter/bombers had much greater capabilities especially when teamed with the converted jet propelled C-135 in-flight refueling tankers. We were the first outfit to fly non-stop across the Atlantic Ocean. Previously, aircraft were only shipped. Our mission was to set up three bases in England from which we supported the war effort in North Korea.

On the day Frank and I arrived at Wethersfield Air Force Base by bus, we located where we would be living, dropped off our baggage, checked to see when and where we would be working. We decided to check out the local people and surroundings since we were not scheduled for any work for several days. We did not waste the opportunity. We grabbed a cab which was readily available. We first traveled to the little village of Wethersfield, very quiet, so we traveled to the town of Braintree, a little better. Then we traveled to Colchester, in Essex. We were told Colchester was the oldest town in England. There was a Roman wall still intact around the original town and the town had a beautiful central park with a castle built on top of an older Roman castle. Frank and I were enjoying the scenery. The people all seemed helpful and friendly. We inquired of a young couple near the bus stop who told us we could freshen up in the men's room. There was a male attendant who went out and purchased razors, soap, etc. and advised us that a Scottish Black Watch regiment, just back from battle in North Korea, was now stationed in Colchester. They were holding a dance at the local corn exchange. He told us how to get there so off we went. Once we arrived we looked inside. It seemed all the women were on one side of the dance hall and all the soldiers in their kilts on the other side of the room.

We didn't know it at the time, we didn't know what to expect, but we bought a ticket and went to the side of the ball room where the women were. Everyone was trying to guess who we were. Up to this time, no Americans had been seen in Colchester. They guessed we were Germans, but we spoke English. We had to tell them we were American Airmen newly stationed at Wethersfield. Frank and I were the only men dancing. The women kept cutting in. We danced until the corn exchange closed, said our goodbyes and took a cab back to the base. What a night! What an introduction into a country neither Frank nor I ever visited in the past. We were told that those dances occurred every Saturday night. We spread the word and before long many airmen attended these dances

The base had to provide police (town patrol) to control the Airmen when they came to Colchester. We became friendly with Black Watch soldiers and admired their service, hand to hand combat with a reputation for outstanding bravery in the face of the enemy.

They wore big boots with cleats in their soles. They were often seen marching on those cobble-stone streets in Colchester, very impressive. They were far from their Scottish homeland, there in Colchester, they were real men! **Those kilts are no joke!** They told us the North Koreans had no Air Force and only the first barrage of Korean fighters had weapons. The second barrage depended on the first barrage being killed so that they could have a weapon also.

Next we had to get our base in shape, readiness meant everything. There were so many firsts with this outfit but I know now this was the best outfit ever. Wherever I went, I was asked to join the pistol/rifle teams to compete with other units. We began to do quite well in competition and I was recognized for my shooting ability. Sometimes I was asked to teach. Often I thought back to the days with my friends from Tamaqua and my old .22 caliber pump action Remington rifle. The Scottish Black Watch told us that the cold war with North Korea probably would not last too long because they were not equipped for war.

I met and started dating the woman who would make me forget all other women, a woman I wanted to have all my children with, the woman I would marry. After we started dating, she informed me that she remembered me from that first day Frank and I came to the corn exchange.

The 20th FTR BMR wing was made up of three FTR BMR Squadrons, each capable of operating independently. The 79th FTR BMR Squadron went to Bentwaters Royal Air Force Station in England with their compliment of B-45 jet bombers. The 77th and 55th FTR BMR Squadrons, with their compliments of F-84 fighter bombers went to Wethersfield RAF Station with the 20th fighter/bomber wing headquarters. I was an Air Policeman with the 77th and it was thought that we would later go to another RAF (Royal Air Force) Station in England. That never happened. Instead, the 55th and 77th Air Police joined to become the 20th Air Police Squadron.

It was exciting. We were making history. Jet aircraft were quite new. We had T-33 trainers assigned which had previously seen service, as our first jet fighter planes, known as Shooting Stars. We had F-84's jet fighter/bomber aircraft and we had KC 135 jet tankers which were reconfigured passenger/cargo aircraft with in-flight refueling capabilities. We also had fixed wing propeller C-47 passenger/cargo aircraft known to be most dependable and reliable aircraft, referred to as, "The work horse of the Air Force" or "Goonie Bird".

The 20th left Langley on the U.S.S. Greely. After a bad nine days crossing the Atlantic, we arrived at South Hampton, England and rode buses to Wethersfield.

Soon after arriving at Wethersfield, rumors circulated and there were articles in British newspapers leaking secrets about Americans bringing atomic bombs to England. The British people started showing up along our fences and gates to speculate and watch our aircraft fly overhead. Mock dog fights took place over Wethersfield. Sometimes British aircraft would take part and occasionally they would land. Many English observers thought that the wing tip (fuel) tanks were atomic bombs and worried that they might accidently fall off causing the destruction of their country. Actually the very shape of the bomb was classified and although loading was practiced, I'm not aware that our aircraft ever flew while loaded with atomic bombs.

These days were very exciting at Wethersfield. We had Doc Blanchard, a Major assigned to the 20th. He was one of the so-called Galloping Horsemen of Army Football fame. We had a Major, I think his name was Krupneck, who flew with a cocker spaniel dog. Major Krupneck held the record for logging the most jet flying hours. It was said that his dog had more jet flying hours than any other assigned pilot. Major Krupneck had a T-33 trainer at his disposal as well as his F-84 FTR BMR to help him maintain his record. He was often seen experimenting with his T-33 trying to solve safety problems when it became apparent pilots were killing themselves due to their poor judgement and their fear of the aircraft ejection system. Another unforgettable man was Sgt. Ed Goddard. He was my flight Sergeant who was well known and appreciated by everyone who knew him. He made a tough job almost pleasant.

Tsgt. Tooley was another unforgettable character. He survived the Japanese Death March as a prisoner of World War II. He brought a new Plymouth automobile to England and lost it in a poker game. I sold him one of my old cars so he could get to work. We had to learn to drive our left hand drive vehicles on the right side of the road.

Then there was my buddy, Airman Westfall, who had a speech impediment due to a cleft palate. He could make you feel so foolish when you did not understand what he said. Another thing about Westfall was his real fear of cats. In the bunk house after work he'd find a cat on his bed, put there by his buddies to get his goat. He would stand outside screaming for someone to get that damn cat out of his bed.

Could anyone ever forget Airman William Boyd? Willie, as everyone called him, was short, strong, black and so funny. He came from Mitchel with Frank Williams Abbey and I. He could light up your day with his humorous ways. A particularly funny act of his was his portrayal of a beggar looking for hand-outs on pay day when men lined up to receive their pay. I never saw Willie spend a dime. I'm sure he went home fairly well off.

We all remember the Blue Bell Pub in Braintree. The train and bus station, double deck buses, warm beer, lime and bitter, malt beer, the dart boards, buses that stopped on every corner, their taxis, the red phone boxes, homes and stores with no refrigeration, hanging meat to cure and sawdust to cut grease on the butcher's floor; fish and chips, steak and kidney meat pies, no central heat, honey buckets, a lot of rabbits; London, The Palace, Westminster Abby, Parliament, The Quid, the pound, ten shillings, a shilling, the crown, six pence, and the "ha penny"; the men who wore coats, ties, vests and changed collars with a button to fasten it to their shirt even when digging trenches and who rode bikes for so many miles. Remember the people who when answering the phone say, "Are you there"?, express anger by saying, "You needn't be so cheeky", refer to schedule as "sheadule", and who refer to a period of two weeks as a "fortnight". They say they will "knock you up" when you want to be awakened. For the most part their meals were very bland, but how I miss their roast beef, when you could get it. Their Yorkshire Pudding, Mince Pies and fish and chips wrapped in a newspaper.

Yes there were some differences. We were paid in script so our money would not end up on the black market like the booze, cigarettes, candy, sugar, nylons, butter, many of which were still on ration in England. We heard a request for "Gum Chum" and a song like "What the hell are we (British) fighting for, the Americans won the war".

We, the 20[th,] had plaques made by the British to include our "Victory by Valour" motto. There are a lot of plaques floating around with the British version of the word VALOR on them. Our car windshield became the windscreen, the hood, a bonnet, the fenders, mud guard, the trunk, a boot, the tire, a tyre.

For the most part there are no language barriers but be prepared should you visit one of their hotels or their famous bed and breakfast homes, and you're asked what time you want to be knocked up in the morning. Expect someone standing over you with a cup of tea when you're awakened.

There were some ugly American stories, but for the most part, we loved the British and they liked us. We made many friends, have wonderful memories and married a lot of their women. No wonder they're our best allies.

Frank married the girl he met at the corn exchange. Approximately fourteen months later, on June 6, 1953, five days after Queen Elizabeth's Coronation, I married my wife.

On April 25, 1954, our first child, a daughter, was born. As soon as I could, I started her training to ride a pony. We rode together at the stable where she took riding lessons. I was so proud of her. She was taught to care for her pony. I bought her a riding helmet, riding breeches and boots, gloves, etc. She didn't appear to fear anything she was asked to try to further her training. I often thought that her instructors were pushing her too quickly.

I spent as much time with her as I could. Due to pregnancy problems, I'd have seven years with her before any more children arrived. I taught her to swim, we hiked and rode ponies or horses, kept a dog for her almost from birth. I spoiled her to say the least.

The three of us returned to the USA on the good ship Upshur, arriving in New York City in April, 1955. I had purchased a new Ford Fairlane hardtop Victoria, black in color, for pick-up in New York City, tax free. I had a little problem driving on the left side of the road after four years of driving on the right side. In England, I had a 1933 Austin, four cylinder motor, on rural roads. Now I'm in New York City with a new 1955 Ford Fairlane hardtop, lots of fun. I made a few mistakes but we made it back to Tamaqua without any accidents.

After a few days at home, I returned to McGuire Air Force Base for discharge or reenlistment. I reenlisted for six more years figuring that there would be little temptation to leave after I had ten years invested. I got my base of choice and a down payment on my first house in Hempstead as a reenlistment bonus, from where I would be working at Mitchel Air Force Base.

My new wife and child loved military life. The new car and new house were almost completely furnished with donations from every family member. Some of the things had to be repaired, some needed to be replaced immediately. The TV, a big square box, was just coming in style. We bought the T.V. new.

The new house had radiant heat throughout. It was nice and warm for our child. The new car sat in a one car garage. Everybody was happy and comfortable. I enclosed our fifty foot by one hundred foot lot with a chain link fence and got a dog for our child. I liked my job, got promoted and worked the control center in a confinement facility which received all prisoners from Europe with over a six month sentence and a dishonorable discharge. I was chosen to return a prisoner to Germany under guard for retrial. I took a couple of weeks' vacation so that when my prisoner was delivered safely, I could explore Germany because it was my Fatherland and I knew nothing about it. I visited a castle on the Rhine River. There was a fun festival going on with a shooting competition. The target was in the shape of an eagle and the object was to shoot until you missed. To win you had to shoot at a wing until it fell off. Right up my alley, I won the competition, which paid for the presents I brought back for my family.

I also rode on a barge along the Rhine River and toured Hamburg, Germany. I found everything just about as interesting as could be.

Soon after I returned from that trip, I learned that headquarters was looking for volunteers to sign up for an assignment at Wethersfield. I knew my pregnant wife would like another four year assignment that would allow her to live in Colchester with her Mother, Brother and Stepfather. She was thrilled that within our first ten years together, she would spend eight years in her old hometown. Right after she arrived in England, she had our stillborn son. This event was the biggest disaster of our lives together thus far.

My wife was pregnant, my daughter, Faith, was four, and I was driving an American 1955 Ford Fairlane. I got assigned to a Communications Satellite Base, (High Garret), near Braintree. The duty was good. There were only two posts a gate and a door inside the communications building. There were two Security Police in dress uniform from the 20th Air Police Squadron for each shift. Neither post was busy and each time I worked the gate I spent most of my time shining my black '55 Ford. People who didn't know who I was just referred to me as "the guy with the shiny car". My Brother, my mentor, asked to use my hunting shotgun while I was serving in England where he knew guns were illegal. I said of course. I would only have to store them. Three years later, I was flown home on emergency leave. I was shocked to learn a shotgun blast ended his life. I flew home for his funeral. I was completely shocked by the news. I had dreams that he and I might be partners in business when I retired. Those dreams were now gone forever. He had used my shotgun to end his life. It was in the hands of police, good riddance.

In April, 1961, I re-enlisted and on June 1, 1961, my beautiful daughter, Roberta, was born with a full head of dark hair, brown eyes and dark skin like her Dad. She was a wonderful addition and the last of our children born in England.

I sold my shiny '55 Ford to a very happy Sgt. at Wethersfield for almost half of what I paid for it in 1955. I ordered a 1961 Jaguar from the Base Exchange, toured the Jaguar factory and watched while they finished building it.

I received orders reassigning me to Grand Forks Air Force Base, Grand Forks, North Dakota where my wife's sister lived with her ex Air Force husband and daughter for the next four years. My wife spent twelve years close to her family during my twenty year Air Force career.

The move from the USA disturbed my wife's pregnancy and hemorrhaging robbed us of our full term son who is buried in Colchester, England. Colchester was an easy commute and a beautiful town. London was close (40 miles) and nice to visit. Places such as Museums, Madam Tussauds, Piccadilly, Trafalgar Square, etc. The seaside resorts of Brighton Clacton on Sea were all worth visiting. Another impressive sight to visit was the American cemetery at nearby Cambridge. The Americans buried here were our brothers responsible for the close relationship we share with the British then and today.

Just prior to our family of four about to leave England for the second time, I purchased a new 1961 Jaguar Sports Coupe. I went to the factory, got a tour and received my new car as it came off of the line. That was quite a thrill, but it didn't last long. I had to drive it to South Hampton, England and put it on a ship. We didn't travel by ship this time. We flew back from England and I had to pick up my new Jag in the States upon arrival. I now had ten years of service in the U.S. Air Force. Again, I re-enlisted for six more years.

My wife's sister was discharged from the British Army and she flew to North Dakota to join, then marry the ex-U.S. Airman she met in England. It had been previously arranged. He also was discharged from The United States Air Force and they were living in Grand Forks, North Dakota. My wife's sister began writing to her Mother who shared those letters with my wife. She wrote of her life in North Dakota in glowing terms. It sounded as though it was a perfect story book life; a lavish home, a big successful businessman husband, etc.

When I checked things out, I learned there was a Grand Forks Air Force Base where they were living. When I inquired of my wife if she might enjoy living there also, she replied emphatically yes!

When I arrived first to arrange for living quarters for my family of four, I found her sister pregnant and her husband pumped gas in a gas station. They were living in the Valley Ho Trailer Park in a mobile trailer.

On June 19, 1963, the Supreme Court of the United Sates handed down a decision which reversed the course of American life and politics. It revoked practices accepted and honored since earliest Colonial times. It ignored Presidents established by Founding Fathers, The Constitution, and the court itself. It ruled that bible readings in public schools were unconstitutional.

I was astounded as were millions of other Americans. How could this be? An action simply can't be good and proper for two centuries and become illegal overnight because a few people object to it. When school shootings and mass murders shocked the nation a few decades later, people wondered what had gone wrong.

I purchased a mobile trailer just to get a space in the same Valley Ho Trailer Park as my wife's sister. After my family, accompanied by my youngest sister arrived, I traded the trailer I bought for a new much larger mobile home. I had to car pool about forty miles to get to the Grand Forks Air Force Base where I would be working. But I didn't mind because I traded a refrigerator that would not fit into the mobile home when it arrived for an old Studebaker. The Jag was not suited for car-pooling. It turned out a Jag is not suited to the temperatures in North Dakota. The Jag had a flat windshield. It was very frigid, blustery weather. The wipers were blown off of the windshield by the wind. I had to install a heater and plug the car in to start the car. I woke up one morning to find all four tires flat on the ground. The tire expert explained that those fancy tires were made of real rubber that froze and burst.

I really don't have much more to say about North Dakota. My wife's sister had a baby girl. They visited and often talked. Fishing was good when everything was not frozen. We had to carry emergency equipment in our cars in the event you got stuck off base. The roads were raised so the wind could blow the snow off of them. It saved on plowing but if your car slipped off the road, you were buried in deep snow. There were no mountains or trees. Many of the roads are just gravel. Temperatures often reached the stage where bare skin would freeze in under a minute. My wife had another miscarriage but then finally had our final daughter. Our family had grown to five and we made the decision not to have any more children. My wife finalized it with my blessings. Our new daughter was the best offering we had in North Dakota and we named her after her grandparents.

As soon as our new daughter was able to travel, we gladly left Grand Forks in our new Cadillac for a vacation in Tamaqua before reporting to our new assignment at Vandenberg Air Force Base in California. This turned out to be the best assignment of all; warm weather year round, forty miles of beaches and mountains, a warm breeze coming off of the ocean, keeping us comfortable day or night. We lived on base and bought horses to enjoy at a beautiful saddle club on Vandenberg Air Force Base. Vandenberg was one of the few places in the world where we could just gather abalone, whose flesh is so delicious and the inside of the shell looks like beautiful Mother of Pearl. It's often used in making beautiful jewelry. Fishing was good right on base. This base was a showplace for foreign and domestic dignitaries. This is the only base where missiles are launched for military testing and/or commercial satellite purposes. This is where I come in, after I arrived. An old buddy transferred in from Strategic Command Headquarters.

Harry the Horse Maltman now held the highest enlisted rank in the Air Force. It didn't change him one bit. He was the same old Harry the Horse, just like a father to me. He was thrilled to hear I owned horses at the Saddle Club. He often visited me there to play with the horses or to talk about the old days. It was Harry who got me the most desirable position in the law enforcement field. He made me the supervisor of the Missile Control Center. I supervised approximately fifty men responsible for security and safety of missile launches. The military testing of missiles were launched unannounced. Men and missiles had to perform as required to hit a target in the bay of an island off shore. If things went wrong, the missile headed inland. The command would be given to self –destruct. In these cases we were responsible for security and safety would take cover for protection from falling debris or flaming solid fuel particles that were very hot. If you took shelter in a low spot, the flaming solid fuel might come rolling right at you. If it landed in the ocean it might boil for hours before it stopped.

We did whatever was necessary to search the designated launch site thoroughly to insure that it was safe to launch. In the case of a military missile launch, we had to do it secretly to avoid alerting the underground missile crew that the launch was eminent. An alert to launch had to be as unexpected as possible in order to be a successful test of their ability. We sometimes used helicopters to search difficult shoreline areas.

A commercial nighttime launch was a sight to behold. Spot lights, used to light up the site, made it appear somewhat like a movie set. When a satellite was launched the missile is launched off of the surface among much fanfare, flames, etc. Something few persons will ever experience in their lifetime. I felt privileged to be a part of it all, Right up front, I was one of the last persons to give the ok to launch.

When a test missile was successfully launched into the bay of that off-shore island, it could be successfully recovered, refurbished and used again and again.

At Vandenberg, on duty or off duty, everything was so pleasurable; helping to organize a horse show at the Saddle Club or a picnic at one of the many picnic areas, riding the horses with friends and family along the shore. The salt water was so good for the horses feet and legs and the resistance of the water strengthened horses legs and bodies; riding in canyons or mountains, never leaving the confines of the base.

Leaving the base, traveling along the shore line, we could visit Disneyland, Hollywood, Movie Theaters or movie lots, Tijuana, Mexico, Venice Beach, Santa Monica Pier, Knots Berry Farm, Santa Anita Race Track or go north on the same highway to San Francisco, Yosemite Park and so many interesting places to visit.

I earned a lot more college credits from Santa Maria College at night while stationed at Vandenberg. I obtained the Outstanding Strategic Air Commands Educational Award while stationed at Vandenberg Air Force Base, California. My parents were happy I kept my promise in that regard.

My wife's Mother visited her oldest daughter in Grand Forks, North Dakota, then wanted to visit our family. I paid for air fare to Vandenberg. She complained that while visiting my wife's sister, she and her husband quarreled constantly. She loved California, as I said. Vandenberg was a show base. She watched a missile being launched. We took her to Hollywood and Disneyland. She enjoyed the horses, the Saddle Club, our children, the mountains, canyons and beaches at Vandenberg Air Force Base. When she arrived back at her home in England, she sent us a copy of a full page local newspaper article with pictures taken to describe her visit and gifts from Hollywood and Disneyland. Pictured also were my wife, daughter and grandchildren and one with our beloved horses and Brandy, our dog.

I disappointed myself though, because I obtained the college credits I needed to attend officers training. I was too old to attend. I blamed the personnel at base records for not informing me of that fact, knowing that was my goal.

My friend Harry the Horse, during one of his frequent visits to my stable, informed me that his son was badly wounded while serving in Vietnam. I could tell Harry was very upset. He told me that he and his wife were planning to visit him at Walter Reed Hospital as soon as he arrived from the war zone.

After Harry's son arrived back at Harry's home on Vandenberg, Harry became concerned about his refusal to deal with his wounds, particularly an arm, which was incapacitated.

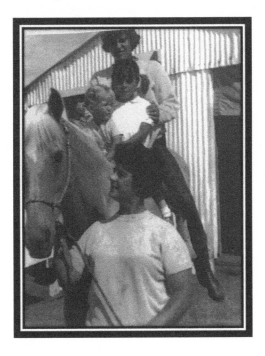

When I found out that my family and I would soon be transferred to Ankara, Turkey, Harry asked if he could purchase my holdings at the Saddle Club. I knew Harry was thinking that he might get his son to take an interest in the horses and the Saddle Club in general. Although I would not be leaving for quite a while, I agreed to the transfer right away.

I was able to witness Harry's son come alive, which was very rewarding. It's amazing what running your hands over the beautiful warm bodies of a couple of horses does for a would-be cowboy.

It was hard for my family to say good-bye to our horses, Harry, his son, the Saddle Club, the missile crew I led, Vandenberg Air Force Base and California. The Air Force had a way of taking care of us no matter what the situation was.

We were informed that our Cadillac Sedan with an eight cylinder engine would not be suitable for use in Turkey. A six cylinder engine in a station wagon would be more suitable for use. We were informed that after six months after our arrival, we could expect culture shock due to the lower standard of living in Turkey.

After a very long flight by air, my family of five and Brandy, our dog (Australian Shepherd), arrived and we were taken to a hotel under contract with the United States Air Force in Ankara, Turkey and managed by Turkish personnel named Marihaba, which means hello.

I was anxious to find suitable quarters so we could accept our family belongings shipped from Vandenberg. Having arrived, it was important to have as many family belongings to surround ourselves with as much as possible I was lucky to find a first floor apartment in the luxury section a few blocks away from the American Embassy on Kennedy Street and only a few blocks from the hotel where single Air Force personnel were billeted and where I would be working. There were four flights of security police to cover twenty-four hours which were switched every three days. I commanded one of these four flights. I was the ranking member. When I realized that I out ranked the Airman running the investigation section with an office in the lobby of the hotel, I approached my new Commander and demanded transfer and to be put in charge of the investigation section. The Commander consulted with the ranking enlisted man in his squadron, who disagreed. It seemed that I had lost the battle if the current Airman in charge had more experience, as they claimed, until I pointed out to the Commander that the investigation section had an unfavorable rating during the past no-notice Strategic Air Command inspection which reflects on the Commander's evaluation. I asked for the opportunity to correct the problems in the investigation section. The Commander agreed.

The apartment I chose to live in was the best choice I could have made. The one balcony and all the windows could not be reached from the ground. Turkish people are afraid of dogs. It's because the only dogs they've ever come in contact with were vicious Shepherd dogs used to fight wolves in defense of their flock. Turks cut the ears off of their dogs at birth so they are not weakened by loss of blood in their ears. They place spiked collars on their dogs throats for their protection.

When Turkish people came to our front door, our only entrance where we might be reached, they would knock on the door. Brandy, our dog, would bark and when we answered the door, our visitor would disappear. There were a lot of Gypsies that would come into town. Often they had a bear on a leash, wearing a muzzle. Their intent, if they could get our attention, was that we would come out on our balcony to be entertained by wrestling the bear for donations of a coin. Gypsies were fascinated and there had been incidents where they kidnapped American blonde children. Our youngest daughter was blonde.

When the Turkish people laid pipe, they would lay sewage and drinking water pipes in the same trench. We had running water but we couldn't use it except to flush a toilet which was a hole in the floor in a closet. There were no traps in the pipes to prevent smells from backing up into your apartment.

We had an American Base about twenty miles from our home where we had to go and haul our safe water.

During our next Strategic Air Command (SAC) inspection, my investigation section was rated outstanding and my Commanders' next evaluation reflected it. My Commander was so pleased that he wrote me an outstanding evaluation and he got me the Non-Commissioned Officer of the Year Award from the whole Turkish command.

The reason why our presence in Turkey was so important was because no Russian war ships could leave Russia without passing through narrow Turkish straits. Their movements were closely monitored constantly. Another reason our presence was important to the United States was because we had Air Bases close to troubling Middle East countries for our military air craft. While in Turkey I was also distinguished for working with crack narcotic teams from Istanbul and Ankara, one of the reasons why other narcotic agencies wanted my services in the future my assignment to Turkey was the first close connection to Muslim people. It was most enlightening. I found a Muslim artist whose talents provided me with portraits of my parents and family in oil on canvas.

mother and dad

We said good-bye to all our American and Turkish friends at the end of my tour. I headed for my last duty tour with the United States Air Force at Ellsworth Air Force Base in Rapid City, South Dakota.

I bought a house on Hazle Street in Tamaqua for my family to live in until I retired from the Air Force. This house was one block away from where my parents lived. Reassured that my family was safe and secure, I traveled by automobile to Ellsworth Air Force Base. I arrived soon after my new Squadron Commander arrived. His first encounter he found everything wrong. He was not happy. He woke everyone in his new squadron and he immediately fired the Security Police Flight Commander who was on duty the first night he arrived. As luck would have it, he fired my old buddy Frank who served with me at Mitchel Air Force Base, New York, Langley Air Force Base, Virginia, twice at Wethersfield Air Force Base, England and now here he was again at Ellsworth Air Force Base, South Dakota.

Our new Commander complained to everyone about the sad state of his new organization. Looking for help from anyone, when he looked at my record for turning the investigation section around in Turkey, along with other records on newly assigned men on his desk and he decided I was the man he needed. I was ordered to report to him. I did so in a military manner. I had talked to Frank in the meantime and I did not know what to expect. I felt bad for Frank. His family was broken and he was close to retirement like I was. I helped him when I could. The Commander gave me everything I wanted. I had my pick of any man in his command, any vehicle and/or piece of equipment, the ability to hire or fire anyone. When I accomplished what the Commander considered satisfactory, I put in my request for retirement. The rules say you must submit your request six months in advance and once submitted you can't change your mind.

In the meantime, Muslim terrorists were hijacking the pride of the American commercial fleet, the first of 747 double deck aircraft, capable of crossing oceans in half the time with record passenger and crew capacity. The President at that time was Richard M. Nixon. He was ordering every military branch of the service, the FBI, Secret Service, OSI, Treasury, etc. to provide their most qualified personnel to be assigned to the Federal Aviation Agency as commissioned Deputy Sky Marshals on a temporary basis until his government could train replacements. This was to be a new organization forming to counteract hijacking for the first time ever.

When my Commander got the President's order, knowing I was ready to retire, he told me he was happy with the job I had done for him. He asked me if I'd like to be recommended to become a Sky Marshal. He and I both thought it was a good idea for me in my position with the possibility of obtaining the experience and a permanent position upon retirement.

CHAPTER 3

The FAA Commissioned United States Deputy Sky Marshal

After submitting my intent to retire with over twenty years in the United States Air Force, Division of Law Enforcement, I was selected from the most qualified men at Ellsworth Air Force Base in South Dakota, as ordered by the President of the United States, Richard M. Nixon, to report to McGuire Air Force Base for specialized training.

The most important part of our training that instructor's had to determine initially, prior to providing any other training, was firearms accuracy. It had to be established that sky marshals could hit a target under extreme conditions. Mock aircraft were used to simulate passengers and crew, considering all of those vital conditions/elements which would be present during any emergency we might be expected to neutralize.

The very next thing to be determined by a psychological examination and a background investigation of each sky marshal selected. The government wanted to insure that all sky marshals could be trusted to do the job they selected them to do. Already skilled in unarmed defense, I was mentally and physically fit from years of exercise, so our instructors only touched on those things we weren't trained in. The technique of deactivation and/or disarmament of explosives. We received training on the specific seven forty seven I would fly on. We knew the most vulnerable areas. We knew all her secrets. We knew the areas which could best withstand any violence, etc. We learned procedures that took place at crew briefings. How we would interact with passengers, air crew and ground crews. We were issued cash (U.S. currency), two passports (one official, one unofficial). The official to be used for our official duties when or if necessary to identify ourselves. This one had to be eaten in unfriendly territory to avoid being shot as spies. The unofficial passport was used for all other purposes. We were also provided with a credit card, used only to buy passenger tickets. In addition, we were instructed that we would be expected to select our own team members to fly with. It was suggested that we choose carefully. Our lives may depend on them at some later date. We were then given a flight schedule listing locations all over the world and corresponding flight numbers. Because I had a military haircut, I was also issued a wig.

I was now serving my country as an undercover commissioned Deputy United States Sky Marshal with a mission to protect commercial aircraft crew and passengers from air piracy. My only weapon was a Smith and Wesson .38 caliber stainless steel revolver and a belly holster loaded with Supervell ammunition. Supervell ammo because it had less penetration and caused less damage should a bullet pass through a targeted hijacker and hit a vital part of our aircraft.

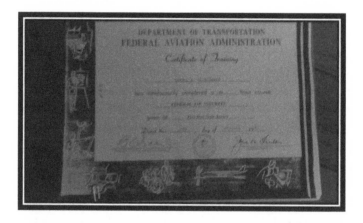

This was the first time in my career that I was instructed to shoot to kill without giving any warning. This was the hardest lesson to learn. It was only when you realized the vulnerability of a 747 airliner with 350 passengers and crew while in flight, that we realized how very necessary it was to eliminate all threats immediately. We were trained in ways to use pilot or crew to gain an advantage over terrorists on the ground or in the sky. We knew how to get messages to one of us or any crew member.

I never doubted that we were at war with terrorism. We were the first (original) Sky Marshals. We were on the front line of that war in the earlier seventies after Muslim terrorists destroyed several of our best commercial aircraft and terrorized our people by hijacking our people and our aircraft to their deserts and destroyed. In twenty sixteen, we have been led by a president who still will not recognize terrorism for what it is.

As far as my team was concerned, we had no real problems. We heard from Intelligence quite often concerning certain passengers that needed to be watched, etc., but we never shot anyone.

In the 1972 Presidential campaign, Democrats, out of power after holding the White House for the last 28 of the past 40 years, tasted blood. Their attacks on Nixon increased. They demanded his impeachment, accusing him of masterminding the Watergate break-in and covering up for his aides. An anonymous informer known only *as "Deep Throat", provided daily disclosures. Partisan politics at its worst blocked legislation in Congress. The beleaguered President had few supporters, at least in public. His abrasive personality had made many enemies even in his own party. Finally, rather than risk impeachment, Nixon went on television to announce his resignation effective August 9, 1975. He did not admit any criminal wrong-doing. The controversy, he said, had reached the point "where I am no longer able to govern." It was a sorry exit for a man beset by his own personal demons. Nixon was the first American President to resign his office. Vice- President Gerald Ford succeeded him and a month later, granted Nixon a full pardon. Nelson A. Rockefeller, a four term Republican Governor of New York, was appointed and confirmed as Vice-President. Thirty years after Watergate, "Deep Throat" revealed himself. He was Mark Felt, Deputy Director of Edgar Hoover's FBI.*

President Nixon's Sky Marshal Program was a complete success. Until September 11, 2001, hijacking aircraft wasn't popular anymore.

President Nixon got into trouble. He lied about some missing tapes. Some of his closest confidants went to jail and he was forced out of office. His enemies didn't want to hear of his successes. We started hearing how the Sky Marshal Program was too expensive. Hijacking Muslims didn't hijack any aircraft from 1971 through September tenth, two thousand one. I felt privileged to be a part of such a successful program initiated by President Nixon that kept Americans safe for over thirty years.

Imagine how I felt when witnessing the twin towers fall one at a time in New York City. The plane that damaged and killed at the Pentagon and the aircraft that crashed in Pennsylvania killing all aboard. Muslim terrorists, armed only with box cutters, caused all that death and destruction witnessed almost entirely on television. Any one of my team members aboard any one of those aircraft would have prevented it. The unthinkable, the thing that could not happen here. War came to America's homeland. It came with startling and destructive suddenness and caught us off guard. The attack shattered our illusions and changed forever our free and easy way of life. It wounded our pride and left us stunned with horror, disbelief and fear.

In one catastrophic second, a bright, sunny Tuesday morning became the blackest day in American History. It was worse than Pearl Harbor, bloodier than any day. The date was September 11, 2001. A small group of Muslim terrorists hijacked four commercial airliners, diverted them from their courses, and used them with all aboard, as guided missiles to attack the nerve centers of America's Financial and Military power. Two of the planes, enroute from Boston to Los Angeles and San Francisco slammed into the Twin Towers of the World Trade Center in New York City. The third, which had taken off from Dulles Airport for Los Angeles, was turned back and crashed into The Pentagon in D.C. The fourth plane failed to reach its target, thanks to the heroism of its passengers. It crashed in a field near Shanksville, in Southwestern Pennsylvania, killing all on board.

Everyone agrees that was the worst attack against our country that has ever occurred. No one thought the Sky Marshal Program was too expensive anymore. I volunteered to go back to duty although I was again retired from the job with the State of Pennsylvania. I was accepted and scheduled to take a physical in Philadelphia. I was called later and told not to report because my pension made me ineligible.

A (D) politician was elected right out of his Church whose pastor, Reverend Wrong, preached from the pulpit that Americans got what we deserved on 9-11-01. "The chickens were coming home to roost", said Wrong. The (D) politician was married and his children were baptized by this pastor. It was said that he was his mentor. The (D) politician made speeches apologizing for American misdeeds. He gave eighty billion dollars to the country of Yemen, (rearranged, it spells "enemy"). Yemen returned the favor by sending us a terrorist on one of our commercial aircraft #253, bound for Detroit with explosives in his underwear, for Christmas one year later.

After his vacation was over, the politician returned to D.C. He stated that attack occurred due to a systematic failure. Someone had to devise that system. He never mentioned that Mr. Funny Pants, terrorist, was seated in the most vulnerable seat in the aircraft. A Muslim seated in that seat bears watching, but there were no Sky Marshals aboard. It was said that it was good that there were no Sky Marshals aboard because if there were Marshalls aboard, the passengers who over-powered Mr. Funny Pants, may not have taken the measures they did to apprehend him. Tell that to the passengers who died along with everyone else in that Pennsylvania field on September eleven, two thousand one.

If Mr. Funny Pants had succeeded with his plans we would have had seen devastation such as was seen in New York City on September eleven, two thousand one. It would have reached into the middle of our country, the Bible Belt, on Christmas. It may have been a Christmas miracle that aided those passengers that subdued Mr. Funny Pants. Keep praying, people, it's our Christian religion that is the best weapon against terrorism.

Removing evidence of our faith that this country was founded on, which (2016), this current administration seems intent on doing, is surrendering to terrorism or anyone else who chooses to be our enemy (Yemen). The Ten Commandments, a manger scene, The Lord's Prayer before school or games, have traditionally been signs of peace and good will. The more we can save of our Bible, the more ammunition to use against our enemies. That includes our own citizens who fight to destroy the religion our country is founded on.

Over thirty years of flying safety with a team of two other men that I chose because I knew I could rely on them in an emergency. Three men, Sky Marshals, were needed each time we flew because of the size of the 747, the largest of its kind. Two in first class because of the two sections and one in second class. We were in a different country every twenty four hours and we had approximately sixteen hours to enjoy time spent or to sleep as needed, before our next scheduled flight.

Some of the most interesting flights were like the one when we left London, England, flew over the North Pole and landed in Los Angeles, California, the day before we left.

Another was when we left Kennedy Airport, New York, for Paris, France. After everyone was seated, we noticed that we were the only passengers on board without name tags. The plane crew took care of that, now we all had name tags. This was a plane with especially assigned crew members, models, who would model clothing during the trip to Paris. All the passengers were winners of a Virginia Slims contest. The trip, a Paris designers show, were the prizes they won. Hostesses changed clothes in the upstairs lounge, came down the spiral staircase, and walked up one isle and down the other, then back up to the lounge to change outfits to keep the show moving.

Another interesting flight was the day before Thanksgiving in nineteen seventy. We flew a giant seven forty seven aircraft fully loaded (three hundred fifty passengers and crew), to San Francisco, California. Then on Thanksgiving we flew the same aircraft back to Kennedy Airport which had no passengers on board. We played games and ate excellent meals and drinks, thanks to the crew.

We bought our tickets with an issued credit card and paid cash for everything else. We attended every flight briefing before each flight to discuss what action was necessary for pilot and crew and whatever the pilot required of us during the flight. Some pilots wanted a Sky Marshal present in the lounge just to the rear of the pilot's cabin during all take offs and landings. We also received a password at these briefings that identified us to avoid exposure during searches.

We met the most interesting people while traveling. Movie stars were the most often first class passengers. I met and talked to a gentlemen who bought a first class window seat for an oil painting he purchased overseas. Another passenger kept me fascinated with his discussion about revolutionizing the home building industry.

Some Sky Marshals were not a part of a team. They were required to fly on smaller planes alone. I heard a story about one such Sky Marshal who disregarded his schedule altogether and used his credit card to buy tickets to destinations all over the world. It was alleged that he got away with it for a long time before being caught and prosecuted. I wonder if he thinks it was worth it now we were given five hundred dollars cash every fifteen days. This money was used for food, taxi's and hotels. Sometimes we pooled our money and rented a suite. We stayed in any hotel we wanted in order to preserve our secret identity. The crews had their hotels under contract. They, the hostesses, didn't like the scrutiny at those hotels. They would beg us to let them come to our hotel to party. I was the only married man on my team so I'd be pressured to let them come to our hotel. It happened a couple of times and boy were they wild. The only way I could avoid it was to get my own room for the rest and privacy I enjoyed and needed. Parties brought too much attention we did not need in our capacity. My other team members agreed and it was over for good.

When we first began flying, right out of the service, we received wigs. There was a story in the news about military personnel being used as Sky Marshals. We didn't want to be identified by our haircuts. The first time I went home after receiving my wig, I surprised my wife who didn't hear me enter because she was using her vacuum cleaner. When she finished she looked up, did not recognize me, got frightened, then realized it was me. My wife did not like the wig.

My hair began to grow like crazy. I couldn't figure how I wanted to wear it. It was all so weird after over twenty years in The Air Force with a military cut.

I was on a flight to San Francisco, California from my home base at Kennedy Airport, Long Island, New York, when I had a discussion with a hostess about my hair. She suggested that I check into one of the better hotels with their own barber shop. When I landed, I did as she suggested and the barber was excellent. He cut my hair the way it grew. When it got messed up, all I had to do was shake it and it fell back in shape. I've never had a haircut like it since, but I can't afford to go all the way to California for a haircut anymore.

While flyting as a Sky Marshal on a flight from Italy to Paris, I met the supervisor of the fifteen hostesses aboard the flight. She used the empty seat on board next to me. As a member of the crew she knew my identity and I was curious about her responsibilities aside from her supervision of the hostesses. She was a very nice looking young woman, tall, blonde, slender but very curvaceous. As we became more familiar with each other she explained that she aids travelers aboard the plane with additional travel plans and assists them in making connections in the terminals. She could, with the help of her computer, issue tickets to assist passengers to continue their travel plans. Once we landed at our destination she told me she lived in California and asked me if I was familiar with Paris. I told her I had only been to Paris a few times and there were so many things I wanted to do while in Paris. She offered to be my guide and stay with me while in Paris. I could not believe my luck. We took a cab from the airport to a hotel on the main Boulevard, Chans de Lise, lined with beautiful trees on both sides lit up at night with the Arc de Triumphe at one end. I don't remember the name of the hotel where we showered, dressed, danced and ate a great meal before retiring for the night. As far as I was concerned, Paris had never been so magical for two lovers. The hostess uniform did nothing for a beautiful woman such as Beverly. The dress she wore that night was gorgeous. We planned a full day at the Louvre Museum, the most famous Museum in the world. We traveled by boat on the Seine River and had our evening meal at the quaint outdoor sidewalk restaurant. I found that I really enjoyed French food. We familiarized ourselves with our past experiences and our respective lives, hers in California. I said I had lived in California and at present I lived on a horse farm in Pennsylvania with kids, dogs and horses. We checked out of the hotel when we went down in the morning and checked our baggage so we could take a cab that night in time for our flight out. We went to the airport together and boarded our plane. It was my turn to fly second class so I found a seat near the rear of the aircraft for our redeye flight back to my home airport at Kennedy. I settled down in my seat. The lights were off and it was dark.

Most of the passengers were sleeping. No sleep for Sky Marshals though. I was just thinking how bored I was going to be on that flight when Beverly showed up and took me farther back to the rear of the aircraft where we made love. When she left to attend to her duties, she said, "Now you're a member of the "Mile High Club". She asked me to wait for her inside the terminal when we land. I said I would. In the terminal I watched as she diligently attended to her passengers. She was finished and off duty about an hour later. She asked me if I was going to be busy for awhile. It was morning and I was also off duty so I told her I had the next fifteen days off, according to my flight schedule. Beverly asked if I could help her find a certain book store in New York City. She said this was the only store that carries the book she had to have. We grabbed the Long Island Express and later a cab. We were in the book store where She found her book. It was a large book containing large colored pictures describing all The positions to engage in the art of love making. Beverly said one of her passengers showed her the book originally and told her where she could get her own copy She asked if I might do her one more favor and help her explore those positions described in her book. I thought it was a long and round- about way to get us back in bed together again, but of course I said yes! We immediately checked into a hotel, ordered room service and settled in for as long as it takes to accomplish our mission. It was an amazing weekend of study and I must admit when we were through we both felt much more educated and thoroughly satisfied. I had explored her body and was more familiar with her than anyone ever before. She had the longest nipples I had ever seen then or since. I saw her off at the airport and neither she nor I inquired if we might see each other again. I kissed her and she waved good-bye. I wondered would I ever see her again. I never did! I think we can know too much about another person, especially a new acquaintance. Maybe someone may benefit from what we learned. Regardless on an airplane with over three hundred fifty passengers, I'm glad Beverly chose me to sit next *to*. I was as happy as a puppy with two tails.

When I came up for discharge, I returned to Ellsworth Air Force Base in South Dakota, retired from The Air Force, then returned to Kennedy Airport and duty as a Sky Marshal. Democrats took Sky Marshals, as the program existed in the past, out of the sky. My supervisors offered me a job in the United States Customs Department which I turned down. I didn't want my family living in New York City. I returned to Tamaqua, sold insurance, refurbished the house in Tamaqua that my family lived in. I then sold it, bought land in Barnesville, Pennsylvania where I 5sed to play as a kid. I hired people to build me a ranch house on a hill with twenty four acres of land. I was not idle. I sold insurance while waiting to hear from the Narcotics Bureau in Pennsylvania.

CHAPTER 4

Pennsylvania Office Of Attorney General
Narcotics Agent, Bureau Of Narcotics

I attended the Narcotics Agent Training Academy at Gannon College in Erie, Pennsylvania. It was intensive, very physical and very interesting. While in training for undercover work, we played many games to build our confidence. For instance, we would follow someone, an assignment, someone whom I had never met before. I would follow that person around the city of Erie, Pennsylvania all day. At times I made it a point to make eye to eye contact. We learned that a simple article of clothing or two, a hat, a coat, a sweater, eye glasses, shades, etc., could shield your identity or protect your anonymity throughout the test. He or she would never leave my eyesight. I made records of their every move or activity. After the test, we would meet the assigned person and they refused to believe that I was the person who was following them all day until faced with the record of their day's activity, photographs, sometimes with both of us in them. They were convinced they never saw me. Before the test began we knew the assigned targets of this test were instructed to take evasive action to lose their tail, so we looked for it and seldom did our trainees loose contact. Although our confidence was built up tremendously, we were warned of the dangers of becoming too confident. There were times it was only that confidence that convinced a bad guy that I could be trusted. Sometimes it was my seeming disinterest that built up the trust needed to get the evidence I needed to successfully prosecute a case. I sat in court many times and learned what was not helpful to a case. I heard fellow agents testify about their need for a controlled substance to make a purchase and their answer to a defense attorney, "My client said he observed you use controlled substances yourself, did you"? Trying to persuade a jury that you were only pretending to use them, I say those looks of disbelief in the eyes of jurors. In my case I never said I needed controlled substances except to use additives and cut controlled substances to double my profit when resold. Any time I was told to use controlled substances as proof of my sincerity, I'd tell the dealer to keep the drugs. Most of the time they came back and I made the buy. I never used or pretended to use drugs. Undercover, think about this: Crime today requires everyone to have cameras everywhere, computers and every other electronic device imaginable. Not just to enable law enforcement or government agents the ability it reaches the stage where it's almost impossible to protect everyone. A cigarette never touched my lips.

Every time I left my home I wondered if perhaps my identity might be discovered or I might appear on camera or some other electronic device. Who knows, I might have been caught on camera more times than even I can imagine. If I had been, I must have done things right. I never made a deal. I stuck to the rules and when the bus came, everyone got their ticket punched! The Holy Bible, Genesis, tells us of God's creation of man in God's image according to His likeness. The Book of Revelation promises the Master of Undercover, Jesus Christ, will return the Alpha and Omega, the beginning and the end. Jesus may have already arrived, walking among us "undercover"! Upon completion the Regional Director at the Erie office invited me to join his team. I graduated second in my class academically and I blew them away on the firing line. I refused, wanting to return to the Barnesville area. My family and I were anxious to begin developing our new property to enable us to obtain horses for my family. Horses, in my opinion, make good babysitters. Horses and drugs didn't mix as I came to believe. Healthy and happy children I knew in the past had good lives growing up with horses involved in their childhood. Those in particular back at the Vandenberg Saddle Club. I saw first- hand how "Harry the Horse's" wounded son developed, caring for and enjoying my old horses.

My oldest daughter graduated from the Tamaqua Area High School and wanted to try her wings with a job in a factory and a rented apartment with one of her girlfriends. She, as I learned from a discussion I had with her, had no interest in college.

Within a year of being on her own, she got married to a young man at the District Magistrates office with only my family present. The explanation as to why he did not have anyone present from his family was that he was adopted and did not get along with his adopted parents. When I asked how he planned to provide for my daughter, he said he was signed up to go into the military.

My other two daughters lived happy lives with the horses I bought for them. They joined a four "H" horse and pony club. The neighbors and I formed an adult riding club. We had trail rides which everyone enjoyed plus we put on horse shows and competed with outside groups.

I instructed my two girls still at home and attending local schools, not to tell anyone what Daddy did for a living. My next older daughter, still at home, told everyone. Her bragging got her known as "the little Narc".

Her school principal contacted me and he told me that the Mahanoy Area School District had a big Methamphetamine, (speed), problem and asked if we could work together to correct it. I agreed that if he would question those students who he knew were involved and inform me, I would do what I could to put the perpetrators out of business. What I learned was that the local doctor in town had a son who could write a better prescription than the doctor could. Everyone referred to the doctor's son as Speed. You gotta be kidding, it couldn't be that easy. We pulled the doctor's DEA Registration with the assistance of DEA. Our boy Speed left town with pressure from his family. The school principal ran and was elected as State Senator. We remained good friends until he was killed in a car accident.

I introduced myself to the District Attorney in Schuylkill County, inquired if he had any problems I might help him with. He informed me that Tamaqua had a big drug problem. Junkies were flocking to Tamaqua for drugs and they were stealing from local business leaders to get money to pay for prescriptions and their presence caused customers to stay away from the business area. This couldn't be happening to my beloved Tamaqua. I learned all the junkies were coming to Tamaqua to see one person. The word was out that you could buy a prescription from my old friend, old Doc Bailey, who was now in his late nineties. His practice got so bad. No one would go to him for legitimate reasons so he resorted to selling prescriptions. I reported to the Schuylkill County District Attorney, told him of my personal connection with Dr. Bailey and asked him if I might handle this situation in the same way that we did in Mahanoy City.

He agreed. I notified DEA and they pulled his DEA registration which permitted him to write prescriptions for controlled substances. He still kept his doctor's license. He could still ride in the back seat on an automobile during parades. People still respected him for his many years of service to our town. A lot of junkies left town and never came back. Some of the local junkies had to get their drugs from the streets now and some were found dead from an overdose, needles still in their arms or cigarettes burned down to their lips.

My supervisors approved of what I had done up until then so they informed me that the tourist town of Scotrun had a similar problem in the Poconos. So off I went to the police station first and learned that complaints they got from downtown were similar to those in Tamaqua, but every time they tried to make an arrest they were faced with drugs which were legally prescribed by a psychiatrist. I found the doctor to be a white female, approximately thirty eight years old with two children and married to the Chief of Medicine at the Scotrun Hospital. She had been or used to be Chief of Psychiatry at the Scotrun Hospital. She began a three county drug rehab program, once operating out of Scotrun Hospital. The junkies created problems in the hospital and she was forced to move the program to the downtown area causing the current problem with drug dealing patients. For patients, for other than medical purposes. As I was gathering evidence, first one of these patients died, then another and another until there was only one left. I quickly arrested her. She waived her preliminary hearing and she sent me a copy of a letter she sent to the District Attorney in North Hampton County. The letter threatened to tell on every lawyer and doctor in North Hampton County if she was going to be singled out for the crimes charged to her. I reported everything to my supervisors but did not receive guidance. Her case sat on the District Attorney's desk for over one hundred and eighty days, then her attorney filed to have the case dropped because she was denied her right to a speedy trial. The doctor left town with one of her patients and I never heard from her again. I later found out that her patients who were taken to emergency rooms with indications of a drug overdose were treated with Narcan for the Codeine. Then after they were discharged from the emergency room, they died from a bolus which formed in their stomach, caused by the Quaaludes which were ingested. Currently a well- known TV doctor is being charged with giving Quaaludes to women in the past to engage them in sex without their consent.

Because of the success I had in the aforementioned investigation, I was sent to work with the Regional Director in the largest city in Pennsylvania, Philadelphia, (the birthplace of our nation).

In Philadelphia, as I recall, we became aware of a group of junkies who discovered a method for obtaining all the drugs they desired using a printing press to print out prescriptions. They would drive around the city looking for other junkies, pick them up off of the street to send into the pharmacies to obtain drugs pursuant to those printed prescriptions using their identities. The deal they made with the street junky was that they would receive a pill or two for their effort.

This was going on all over the city and the volume of drugs of all kinds was tremendous. In this group of junkies, I found some of the most desperate drug addicts of all. I experienced men and women who immediately upon departing from a pharmacy, would fill their syringe from a mud puddle to inject the drugs into their bodies. One junky would overdose, another who had heard a story about urine being used to bring an overdosed person back, would fill a syringe with urine and inject it into an already dead body. Some junkies had difficulty finding a vein because of so much abuse and he'd have to go to a gang member always referred to as "Doc" to get high. Sometimes the only vein not already destroyed was under the tongue or scrotum. We had a drug raid. We formed teams of local police led by one of our Narcotic Agents to spread out all over the city of Philadelphia to pick up the ring leaders along with every junkie who obtained drugs pursuant to phony prescriptions.

I had to use my personal vehicle, a Ford Ranchero, on the job for approximately the first year while working for The Bureau of Drug Control because they didn't have sufficient government vehicles for everyone. I didn't like using my personal vehicle because I didn't like the possibility of being identified by the vehicle I used for work. The government reimbursed me for the expense and I had another vehicle I used extensively for personal business but they were both registered with my real name. I felt more vulnerable and there was also the possibility that my family might unnecessarily get involved with the dangers of my job.

I knew I was on top of the list to receive a government vehicle when one became available, but I kept looking anyway. Finally I learned that there was a government vehicle not being used by the agent it was assigned to. The agent's wife was a school teacher and his duties were strictly administrative so he used his personal vehicle and dropped his wife off at her school each day on his way to work in Philadelphia. The government vehicle sat at the curb in front of his home for so long that the tires were flat. It needed a new battery and extensive service but I finally had a government vehicle for use undercover that matched my undercover identity and my undercover Pennsylvania driver's license. Life was good, it was a rattle trap but that suited its' purpose also. The agent who was the previously assigned agent to drive it, was happy that it was gone from his property and he didn't have to concern himself that he'd ever be accused of using a government vehicle for personal business again.

I only had the vehicle about one year when I was driving through the back streets of Stroudsburg at night and I heard bullets hitting my undercover car. I was very familiar with that sound due to a previous investigation that required me to do extensive testing while in The Air Force Investigation Section to convince a military court of a suspects guilt. I quickly looked in an attempt to determine where the shots were coming from. Failing that, I put the pedal to the metal and screeched tires to absent myself from that area. An extensive investigation was done with negative results. t God wink.

A guy famous for his commercials back in those days promised to paint any car for twenty nine ninety five. His name was Earl Shibe.

He got our business every time one investigation was over to prepare our cars for a new investigation. It was an old Plymouth. I had a local garage to do repairs on government vehicles. He maintained all state police cars too. Since the old Plymouth had been used in previous undercover jobs, I could not be certain that I was the target of an unknown shooter. A new paint job and moving to a new area of investigation seemed to solve the problem. The new paint didn't last long. It began to peel in the breeze while driving and the bullet holes were always there as a reminder.

Next I arrested a woman who received drugs pursuant to a medical doctor's prescription. The District Attorney gave this woman an opportunity to work with us in order to obtain consideration upon sentencing in the case brought on her, when he learned from an interview he had with her, her claim that many doctors provide drugs to her to party with.

Upon my interview with her, I learned she was gay with a girlfriend who had more skills than she did. When I interviewed her girlfriend, I learned that the ringleader, referred to as "Fat Cat", was currently in prison, that he was the brains of the group.

I interviewed Fat Cat in prison. It sounded good. We got him placed into our custody. We rented a room in a hotel to be used as a Central Control Room. The girls followed his instructions as in the past and we began to gather evidence against many pharmacists, pharmacies and doctors they used in the past.

In the past, Fat Cat would, according to the girls, instruct them on how to steal meat from stores to get money to pay pharmacists or doctors. Fat Cat could always get money for meat. These girls would select meat that Fat Cat would order, shove as much as they could up between their legs and walk out of the store. Fat Cat chose the stores to be robbed, the pharmacists, doctors, etc. The girls said that Fat Cat had many more girls that worked for him and all he got out of it was spending money. The enjoyment he got from leading a group of girls and going to their parties in hotels rented by Fat Cat. The woman said, "at parties when they passed out, they would wake up naked and positioned as Fat Cat placed them.

I had to change things around. Obviously Fat Cat was never to leave the room. He remained under guard as long as he was in our control the girls or anyone else would never steal anything. The money needed would come from money provided by our Bureau to pay for drug purchases, informant fees, etc. We sent Fat Cat back to prison as soon as we had enough information as needed. The agents used to guard Fat Cat were needed to go further with this investigation. We needed a female agent to strip search the female informants any time they handled our money, drugs, etc. This would keep them honest and give them credibility if they were ever needed to testify. Informant testimony was only used when absolutely necessary. Our goal was to cut them out and make agent purchases as soon as possible. To give an example of how I used a female informant to a good advantage in an investigation at a pharmacy. The female informant carries our female agent's purse into the pharmacy. They go into the pharmacy together. When the informant goes behind the counter with the pharmacist, she hands the agent her purse back containing the buy money saying, "Here, hold this. I don't want this guy ripping me off." She makes the drug deal and tells the pharmacist that our agent is a junkie she brought along to handle the drugs and money because she, the informant, was out on bail and did not want to go back to jail. The informant asks the pharmacist to give our agent (junkie) the drugs and the informant tells our agent how much to pay for the drugs. The pharmacist asked why would our agent (junkie) do that? Answer: "For a piece of the action. Bye now"! The evidence was good. Our agent received the drugs purchased with our money that she paid to the pharmacist. She could testify in court and her character would never be in question.

Many similar schemes were devised, always being careful not to violate anyone's rights, always important when dealing with high profile perpetrators. Many doctors or pharmacists never make it to court because they usually waive their right to preliminary hearing and the county District Attorney is then facing an attorney representing the practitioner with both a medical and a legal license and background. A deal is normally reached and charges are reduced or are dropped. Get used to it. Most

District Attorneys that are elected to represent the public do not have a medical background. In my opinion, an attorney without a medical background doesn't have a chance against one who does. The AMA or Pharmacy Association can and often does provide their members with good lawyers.

The Regional Director in charge of the Philadelphia office got in trouble concerning funds and evidence was called into the headquarters and fired. I was placed in charge. I immediately did an inventory covering every area of my responsibility as the new Regional Director in our Philadelphia office.

Investigations and arrest of practitioners all over the city were taking place. Some licensed doctors registered to write prescriptions didn't even pretend to be a doctor with a medical practice. Take the case of one doctor who would set up his practice in a strip mall knowing with his reputation for selling prescriptions, he would have his patients flocking to his new door. When other business owners in the same area started complaining about the problems they were having with his clientele, no problem. The doctor would load his desk and some chairs on the back of a pickup truck, move to a new location and wait for his patients to find him. They always did.

The kind of success we were having with high profile criminals doesn't go on very long without being noticed. With a policy that says you break the law, everyone gets their ticket punched when the bus comes! If deals were made, they were made by those people in law enforcement above me.

Philadelphia was a real learning experience for me. I met some really bad people and very good people in law enforcement. Those who appeared to have no training, who could get you killed with their stupidity, and others, you could learn from.

After a very tough operation, one where everything went well, the undercover team was well covered, never in real danger. Surveillance teams did their jobs well. The plan worked well and as a result we had all the evidence, tapes, prescriptions, films, drugs, etc. necessary to make a good arrest and we knew we'd have a good prosecution. Our adrenal glands would be pumping, had us high with excitement just knowing that during our post operation review everyone did their job well and with each report from every participant their excitement added to our own. Even the informants would get caught up in the excitement and they often asked how they could join law enforcement or could they have a badge or even a gun. At times they became over- zealous and were deemed to be useless for further use.

Not so with a friend of mine I use to work with, another agent who I didn't often agree with. He'd tell me of his exploits when we got together, like the time he discovered a doctor's wife was writing her own prescriptions on her husband's pads. He made a deal with the doctor that if he would involve her in rehab. He would make no arrest. The woman died of a drug overdose. Another time he was on surveillance and he was approached by a farmer who offered to help, thinking he might be stuck on the dirt road. He showed him his badge and said he didn't need help. They entered into a conversation and the farmer said he owned the property on both sides of the road and that he'd like to have a trench in the road so his cattle could cross from one side to the other without having to open a gate. My buddy said he did not see why he could not dig a trench. It was just a dirt road. You guessed it. He got called into the office. The farmer got into trouble, He reported that he, my buddy, gave him permission so he did it.

My buddy's wife had health problems and they had to move to Arizona. He got a job working as a Security Officer at a Nuclear Power Plant near Phoenix, Arizona. I visited him in Arizona. He took me horse-back riding on the desert. He said that one of the nearby small towns had drug problems, heard he had been a Narcotic Agent in the past and they asked him if he could help. He said he told them if he had the assistance of one of his informants from Pennsylvania, he would. He said they agreed to fly his informant to Arizona, house him while there, pay him and my buddy a salary they both agreed upon. He said they had a drug raid within one month. He had the town cleaned up. His informant was flown back to Pennsylvania and he is hailed as a hero. I don't know how much of this I want to believe but I figured my old buddy hadn't changed much. He was still making deals. By the way, before I forget, this same buddy was in the middle of that investigation of the Regional Director in Philadelphia. So I don't know how voluntary his move to Arizona was.

The Regional office in Philadelphia was situated in a building that also housed a rehab one floor below our office. After I became the temporary Regional Director I complained. The Regional office in Philadelphia was closed and all of the agents, including me, were transferred to other regions to work under another Regional Director. My new boss liked the new car I was driving better than his so we traded cars. I liked him, he was retired Air Force like me and we got along well. We went through the academy together. I was now in our Kingston office. I had a nice corner office with windows in both directions and we had a State Police contingent in our office. I also enjoyed the interaction with State Police.

During this period my second daughter finished high school.

My wife and I divorced. She moved to Cheyanne, Wyoming to be near an Air Force Base and her sister. She loved the military life and its benefits. I loved the country.

I got full custody of my youngest daughter who loved her life at home and was still in high school. Soon she graduated and I was encouraging her to take her SAT's and get enrolled in a college. She wasn't interested in leaving her horse or her home.

In the meantime, the Bureau was training new agents at Wilson College. This was an all girls' school that the Bureau rented space from. I was sent there as an instructor. OLAY!

They had an Equine Science course and a stable for horses. I asked my youngest daughter if she could study anything she wanted, what would it be? She said horses! I told her to start packing her horse, Cognac. She took her SAT's and made application for Wilson and I delivered her and her horse to Wilson. After a year, she decided to change her major and Cognac, her horse, came home.

I began building cases in my new Region VIII out of the Kingston office. I was in court in Wilkes-Barre assisting an Assistant District Attorney prosecute one of my more important drug dealers that I arrested. The prosecution went well and he was convicted. As this case goes, we try to pyramid our investigations to find and arrest the next highest dealer until we find, investigate and arrest the dealer at the highest level. This is important in the war against drug dealers. The Assistant District Attorney whom I assisted with prosecuting that case informed me that our next case for prosecution was much more important and the court transcript for this case would clinch our case against the next dealer. I didn't even remember looking at the Court Reporter in that first case so I didn't know if I could find him or her.

I went to the Office of the Court Reporter. When I told them what I was seeking, they directed me to the desk of whom I will call Candy. Candy was the youngest, but from what I was told, the most skilled Court Reporter. I told her what I wanted and she informed me that it was impossible. I tried

to persuade her, telling her how important it was. She told me it was the weekend and to finish it in time, she would have to work all weekend. I told her my Bureau would pay her at the going rate and she agreed to do it.

The following Monday I went to Candy's office. She gave me the transcript. I asked her how much I owed her and she asked me to take her out for dinner some night. I agreed, thanked her again, and left. I saw her again during my next trial but this time I looked at her real good. She was a beautiful little thing with a great body but she looked like she could not be older than twenty-one. I was having reservations about my agreement with her. In talking to people at the Court House and learning what a sacrifice it was for her to accomplish what she did for me, I decided I would keep my promise. I learned Candy lived in an apartment two blocks from my office. I told her I'd pick her up at her home on the next Friday night.

I went to her home around seven in the evening and found that her apartment was beautiful. It was obvious she made good money at what she does. She informed me that normally she hires people to type her transcripts. That explains where she gets her money from. One murder trial and she gets enough money from selling copies of the transcript to buy a new car.

I asked her where she'd like to eat. She said she understood I was the new agent in town and that until recently I worked in Philadelphia. I admitted that what she said was true, so she asked me to take her to a nice restaurant in Philadelphia. I said only if you don't lie to me about your age. She said she was nineteen. You also have to agree that we will do no drinking or taking of drugs. She agreed and off we went. It was about an hour and forty- five minute drive. When we got there, the evening was just beginning. She wanted to visit some of the dives I worked in the past. I gave her a tour and she was so inquisitive about everything. Everything seemed so different when seen through her eyes. We finished the evening at a Middle East restaurant down near the docks. There were belly dancers and Middle Eastern music coming from a balcony. She seemed to be enjoying it tremendously.

Candy fell asleep in the car returning from Philadelphia. When we arrived at Candy's apartment, she acted like she was drunk. I knew she had nothing to drink or I did not see her take anything, but she had to be helped into her apartment. It was early on Saturday morning.

Once inside the apartment, Candy came alive. I found myself on her bed, her bare body hovering over me. I felt her moisture falling onto my body and before I knew it, we wer locked into an embrace like one I had never experienced before.

Candy didn't want me to leave, but I had animals to be cared for. On my drive home, I remembered her small breasts. They seemed so firm. I told myself that I had to stay away, she could be habit forming. And she was way too young for me. I did not want to marry any more, especially to someone so young. All my children were older than Candy.

I didn't see Candy for about a week and a half. I was in the court house and Candy caught up with me in the cafeteria where I had gone for lunch between sessions in court. Candy had a girlfriend with her who she introduced as Betty. Betty's father was a doctor and she told me that she had horses all her life. She worked with Candy as a Court Reporter. They were best friends.

On Friday of that week, Candy called me at my office. She wanted to know if I would give her first horse-back ride. She explained that horses were all Betty talked to her about. She remembered that we had a good conversation about horses and she thought how nice it would be to have horses in common with Betty. She said she would respect my wishes.

Candy arrived at my place on Saturday a little before noon. It was a beautiful sunny day. I chose Cognac, a big thoroughbred bay gelding that I trusted with all my children, for Candy's first horse-back ride. I selected a trail which we all knew very well, especially Cognac. It went straight up the mountain to the top. We were both dressed with shirts and jeans without shoes. Candy had flip flops on.

We rode bare back on that big warm bay colored horse on that trail that day. His movement was like music. The warmth of all our bodies seemed to melt together. I could feel Candy's firm little breasts against my back. I then felt my shirt being lifted off and I felt her bare breasts against my bare back. I was thinking that I have to pull off the trail to finish this when I felt Candy's soft, strong hands loosen my belt and open my pants. She then slid around to the front of me and as we traveled up the side of that mountain in a smooth, warm embrace that required nothing from either of us, just the rhythmic motion of a big warm bay gelding named Cognac. I thought, "he'll never tell!"

To say the least, we had a great time horse-back riding that day. We had to retrieve a few items of clothing on our way back down the mountain. I could put Cognac right away. He didn't need cooling down, he had an easy trip and wasn't over-worked. Once Home, I fed Cognac and Candy and I spent the evening and all day Sunday in my bed. I didn't think about how old she was anymore. I considered it the gift of a lifetime and I thanked her for being there.

Nineteen year old Candy approached me when we met in the courthouse one day. She was crying and I could see she was very distraught. I inquired

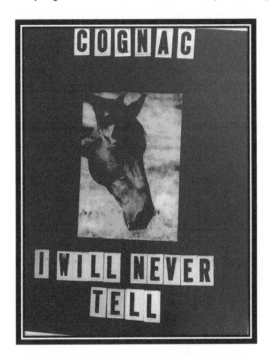

as to what her problem was. I wanted to know why she was crying. It took a while for her to regain her composure but when she did she told me that one of the court's lawyers had her very frightened. She explained that he met her in one of the courtroom halls, pushed her against one of the walls and fondled her.

I wanted to know who he was but she was reluctant to identify him, frightened that she might lose her job but mostly because of the way he made her feel, helpless without the ability to avoid that type of conflict on a daily basis while working for a living at a job she loved and worked so hard to obtain. She wanted to know what I could do to prevent it from happening again. I told her it's better that she does not know what I could do about it.

No matter what I did to resolve the situation, I did not want implacability where Candy was concerned. I promised not to implicate her and she identified her offender. He was head Attorney for a group of attorneys known as Public Defenders. I knew him well because nine out of ten times persons I arrest use their services to defend against my prosecution of them. He referred to my undercover work as barbaric!

I stalked him in the court house until I knew I could have him alone. I grabbed him, shoved him through the swinging empty court room doors, gave him a knee to the groin and before he could call out, I informed him of my purpose. Without identifying anyone, I told him I knew of his illegal activities, reminded him that he was a married man with a responsibility to the county and how quickly that could change now that I was aware of it if it did not stop immediately!

The very next day Candy telephoned in a very surprised, happy voice saying, "He's gone"! She told me that he surprised everyone by announcing his resignation to allow him to enter into his private legal practice. Candy wanted to know what I did. I told her I didn't do anything. That may be true, he could have had resignation on his mind before we had our little talk.

As I write this story, poor Candy has been gone for many years. I still miss her so much. The attorney who attacked her has been doing his own advertising on T.V. I see him often and I'm like my old horse Cognac who is also dead for many years. "I'll never tell"!

Candy told me that she was pregnant, that it happened before she met me. She did not want to talk about it. She asked me to be considerate. She had to take care of everything. She had Betty"s help. Soon after, she informed me the pregnancy was over and she told me she was on birth control.

Candy told me her parents were the happiest couple she knows. Her father was much older than I and her mother's age separated them by a much larger gap. Candy asked me to come to their place for dinner, and we met. Both Candy and her mother were great cooks. Candy's mother worked in another county court house and her father was retired but very active in church. They did seem like a very happy couple.

Before I knew it, Candy had purchased her own horse and boarded it where Betty boarded her horse. She took riding lessons from the owner of the stable. Before long she was good enough to train her own horse. I watched her through it all and joined her, helping her with her horse and tack while she competed. I hauled their horses for them. I brought a group from their stable to Barnesville to compete at one of our shows. It was great fun.

Candy's horse died. It was a great loss but she handled it well and she purchased another better horse. She was even more set on making this horse better or even the best. Those hands that made her so successful at work were magic at the controls of the horse. I thought Candy had something to prove to herself. I guessed it included me.

Candy said she envied my knowledge of our country because she had never been anywhere but Pennsylvania. She was always so inquisitive. I told her to slow down. She was so young. She had a lot of time to catch up. She already had a good respectable job and a good income. Candy had type one Diabetes and explained that she always felt that with insulin injections required from birth, she might not live until she reached old age. That explained her desire to experience everything now. My military retired status provided me with a lot of benefits like free space available travel and board, military air craft, use of military resorts and military bases world-wide.

I promised Candy that if she could manage a thirty day vacation, I would show her my America as I knew it by automobile. I had more than thirty days of vacation accrued so we were half-way there. Talk about eager. It was just a short time and she announced she was ready to leave. I was happy and eager too. She was such a pleasure to be with. We left Pennsylvania on I-80, drove through Ohio, Indiana, Illinois, North through Minnesota's twin cities, West through South Dakota, and checked into the Visitors Quarters at Ellsworth Air Force Base (AFB).

When we were awakened the next morning, I gave her the tour of the AFB. We ate in the cafeteria, left the base, drove through the Badlands and Wounded Knee Indian Reservation. I explained that in the past while in the service, I had to go arrest AWOL Indians at Wounded Knee who were not treated the same as AWOL white people. Because of their heritage, it was expected that they would go AWOL because the draw of their home on the reservation was so much greater than ours. I took her on a tour of Rapid City. I showed her the line on the Main Street where Indians got drunk and where cowboys get drunk. There was a clear division because, believe it or not, cowboys and Indians were still at war. Cowboys resented the fact that Indians on reservations benefited in many ways due to the ancient treaty agreements made many years ago. Everywhere we went, Candy was loved. She just enjoyed everything.

Next we drove through the Black Hills, bought a small Black Hills Gold bracelet and visited Mount Rushmore Mountain, the International Monument to past Presidents

We returned to the Ellsworth AFB, spent another night in the Visitors Quarters. We were awakened the next morning, ate breakfast at the cafeteria and traveled north to Deadwood City, an historical old Western town famous as the city where Wild Bill Cody was murdered while playing cards in the saloon. Until this day, the hand that he held when killed is known as a Deadman's Hand. It's famous for a yearly celebration called Deadwood City Days. Every year thousands of people on motorcycles celebrate Deadwood City Days. I've been there, it's wild!

Candy and I watched a re-enactment with local actors, of the killing of Wild Bill, (he was shot in the back). It was interesting touring this old Western town. There were a lot of horses and cowboys which we always enjoy and a lot can be learned from these old stories from the past. We dressed in Western styles, spending a night in that ancient historical town in a Western style motel, encouraged another romantic dinner and dancing, Western style, and lovemaking Candy style.

Next we drove out into Wyoming's Yellowstone International State Park, visited the Geysers, Jackson Hole, The Grand Teton Mountains, traveling South to I81 where we checked into a motel for the night. The next morning we ate breakfast at the motel, traveled on I81 to Lake Tahoe in California then to Yosemite National Park. Candy was amazed at the size of the Giant Redwood trees that cars could drive through holes carved through those trees. People actually carved homes in these trees. She enjoyed hearing about the Indian Legends, the lakes, half dome mountain waterfalls and the wild animals. We spent the night in a motel in those beautiful mountains. The weather was gorgeous and Candy glowed with pleasure. I never enjoyed visits to these American treasures as much as I did this time with Candy, seeing them through her fascinated young eyes.

The next morning, awakened by the animal sounds, we ate breakfast and drove to San Francisco where Candy and I rode trollies and visited fine restaurants on the pier for great seafood and great entertainment by the seals that live there.

We spent the night in one of the fine hotels in the city that I used to visit as a Sky Marshal. I got a hair cut by a barber who cut my hair for the

first time other than military style. Candy had her hair cut and styled also. She was beautiful! The next day we had a good breakfast, crossed the bridge and traveled South on the coast highway. We visited Hurst Castel and a Seal Rookery. We stopped occasionally so Candy could take pictures of something that grabbed her. Eventually we arrived in Lompoc, California where Vandenberg Air Force Base was. Lompoc is the seed capital of the world. As you approach Lompoc from the top of a mountain road, you can look down over the valley below. You can see the whole valley is covered with gorgeous flowers. Because of our interest in horses, the first place I took Candy was the Saddle Club where I used to keep my horses while stationed at Vandenberg AFB.

After we had our fill of horses, we checked into Visitors Quarters for one week, the maximum time allowed. I had many things planned for Candy while there at Vandenberg because it was such an easy drive to so many interesting attractions in Southern California. Visitors Quarters weren't the fanciest accommodations, but they were more than adequate and they were cheap. I could make purchases in the Post Exchange at fair prices and we could eat good meals at the NCO Club on base cafeteria at reasonable discount prices. Candy enjoyed everything. She got a lot of attention everywhere we went. Even I got a kick out of that. I ran into an old friend that I knew from the Saddle Club when I belonged. He retired at Vandenberg so that he could take advantage of Vandenberg's benefits. I talked him into letting us borrow a couple of his horses so I could take Candy riding on the base.

The next morning after a great evening and a good night's sleep, we arrived early at the Saddle Club and found everything as we were told it would be. We saddled up and rode in the canyons and mountains first, tied up at the NCO Club had a good lunch and finished our ride on the beaches. While riding on the beach I ran into a member of my old Missile Security outfit. I introduced myself and inquired if he was aware of any upcoming missile launches. I knew that he was not supposed to give this information out so I promised we'd never mention it to anyone. I fully understood but it meant a lot to me. He told me everyone still talks about Harry the Horse. He'd heard of the legend. We had a long conversation. He was on guard duty and I got the idea he wanted to keep Candy around as long as he could. He was enjoying the horses too. He told me of a scheduled underground missile launch two days away. I said I remembered the indicated launch pad. We had to get the horses back to the stable, cool them down and feed and water them.

I called my friend, told him his horses were home and well taken care of. I thanked him for everything. We drove to the NCO Club, had dinner and Candy couldn't thank me enough for a wonderful day. By morning, although we were both very tired from a long exhausting day, Candy had me completely convinced that she was a very happy camper.

When we were awakened the next morning, we showered, had breakfast at the cafeteria and traveled South on the coast highway to Venice boardwalk and spent the day there. Candy was fascinated with the lifestyle of the local people. It was so different from anything she had ever seen. Skating, bicycling, roller boarding, surfing, half-naked people on the shore or boardwalk, etc. I had seen it all before but never through Candy's eyes. Another great day, again grateful to be in each other's arms and the warmth we felt for each other. I tried to surprise Candy each day with a new experience.

The next day we were awakened and headed south to Malibu, California. I wanted Candy to see all of the lavish estates so we toured Beverly Hills and ate dinner at the famous Beverly Hills Hotel. We then visited Hollywood and the Grauman's Chinese Theater. She visited Hollywood and Vine and stuck her toes in every movie stars' imprints in the cement. We ended our tour at Pasadena but of course there were no Rose Parades, the wrong time of year. It's only held one time a year, New Year's Day. We drove back North on the Coastal Highway. Candy was amazed at the size of the giant Pelicans who came so close looking for handouts. The highway wound through tunnels and curves. We passed by beautiful estates hanging over cliffs along the shore. We drove close to President Reagan's home and library and the estate of Roy Rogers where his horse Trigger is buried. Candy was all cuddly as I drove back to Vandenberg. I hated waking her up when we arrived.

The next day Candy asked if we could just spend the day on the beach. We slept late, showered and ate breakfast. We then went to an area of the beach to spend the day relaxing. Unknown to Candy, it was missile launch day. I selected an area of the beach where we wouldn't be disturbed but it was a safe area to witness a missile coming out of the ground and hopefully heading out over the ocean.

I showed Candy how to harvest Abalone shell fish with their beautiful Mother of Pearl shells, from the rocks along the shore. She saved several shells to take home as souvenirs. We spent time in the water and relaxing on the beach until we were both frightened by the launch of the missile. We watched it until it disappeared out of sight over the ocean. Candy had witnessed something that so few have ever witnessed. That same day, a famous Canadian Aircraft Flight Acrobatic Team had a demonstration that we also enjoyed.

We were awakened the following morning prepared for another full day of sight-seeing. Nothing was too much for Candy and I was just as enthusiastic. It has been a while since I did everything in the past and never within thirty days.

We ate breakfast and traveled South on the coastal highway to Knott's Berry Farm, an amusement park where we enjoyed the whole day.

We returned to Vandenberg, ate dinner at the NCO Club, slept, had breakfast and traveled south to Mussel Beach, Santa Monica. A group of musclemen entertained us and I gave Candy a tour of the Santa Monica Pier. The diving bell amusement that accepted the baby seal my friend and I rescued was gone. The old dog (Bum) that befriended me was gone as I expected because so many years have passed since the days I enjoyed as a child. Candy appeared to enjoy my reminiscing about my childhood. We watched the boats returning from a long day on the water with their catch of fish. Candy expressed a wish to do that herself someday. Her wish was my desire. I made reservations with the Captain of the boat for the very next day.

After breakfast the next day, we got up early and traveled to the Santa Monica Pier where we boarded the boat for a day of fishing. While we were traveling to the deep water, we were both issued a fishing pole and instructed how to use the bait. When we arrived they shut down the engine and dropped the anchor. Everyone began fishing. There was a nice group on board. Candy was the only woman so she got a lot of attention. She had a guy to bait her hook, a guy to net her fish and take it off of the hook. The fish that we caught were divided among the other men. Candy and I caught a lot of fish and the men all had extra- large catches for the day. We got a lot of help fishing. It was a great experience and a good time was had by all. The men shared their beer with us. We had a ball. It turned out to be quite a party boat, full of good natured people having a good day on the water

and Candy could say she had been deep sea fishing for her first time. She loved all the attention she got that day but I was the beneficiary that night.

We returned to Vandenberg Visitors Quarters for our last night. We ate breakfast, visited the Saddle Club again, said good-bye to all the horses and anyone who was hanging around. We headed south on the coastal highway for the last time. We were going to spend a day at Disneyland before moving on. It was a wonderful day at Disneyland as anyone who's been there can attest to. Candy behaved like a small child unlike someone in her middle twenty's. As old as I was, I still felt like a child. Disneyland, Disney World or Disney Euro, it's all the same. We had a ball thanks to Disney. We had a nice dinner and a good nights' rest at the Disney Hotel.

The next morning we had breakfast and left for the Paramount Movie Lot Tour. When we arrived we rode a trolley through the waters which parted, got swallowed up by Jaws and Candy looked so good in her bikini that she got mauled by Frankenstein and gobbled up by the Wolfman. I got so hungry watching all this that I wanted to devour her also, so I did!

After another glorious night in a motel, we moved on to the famous Santa Anita Race Track. I explained to Candy that the Racing Commission had a drug problem at the Penn National Race Track in Pennsylvania and agreed to pay expenses to train one of our agents the ins and outs of track life. Since I was the only NARC who owned his own horses, I was chosen to work with the Racing Commission Agents who were conducting a gambling investigation at Santa Anita Race Track in California for thirty days. I offered to show her what I learned and give her a tour of the backside of a track, training of a race horse, swimming of a horse until his leg injury healed to keep him in shape, leg wrapping, washing grooming, etc., a meal in the Track Cafeteria with the jockeys' trainers and owners, and a two dollar bet on her favorite horse in any race that day. She recognized some of the owners she saw in the Cafeteria and on the backside of the track as having seen them in movies. Her horse did not win any money. I don't know what she used to make a selection. My chosen horse won because I knew from the description in the racing form that he was related to one of my horses. I won $200.00 on my $2.00 bet.

We found a nice little motel near the track to spend the night together. It had the feel of horses and horse people. Candy was full of questions about the day's activities and the people we met. She also wanted to know why my horse won and hers didn't. I told her that I bred my horse, Sargete, a Quarter horse, to a very good thoroughbred racing horse down at Penn National by the name of "Restless Wind", and named the foal "Mariah Quest:, French for "Quiet Wind", after her daddy who was crippled and was only used for breeding I was attracted to a horse on the racing form whose sire was also named "Restless Wind" and he won. She said I cheated and I was not playing fair. We slept well that night after a busy long day at the track.

After breakfast the next morning we got a good start which proved to be a long desert highway through the rest of California and into Arizona. We only stopped two times to admire the Painted Desert and the Grand Canyon. We were tired of sight-seeing so we ate dinner and stayed at the local hotel. We did a lot of driving this day. We stayed at a nice motel where I often stayed when in Phoenix, Arizona in the past. It was situated at the foot of Camel Back Mountain.

The next day we drove all the way through New Mexico, through the Texas Pan Handle and into Oklahoma. Then we found a nice motel in Oklahoma City near the Cowboy Museum. I had been there before and I knew it was a place that would interest Candy. By now I pretty well knew what interested her.

After a good night in the motel, it was a cozy kind of night, we weren't so tired and we were into each other. I remember thinking I don't want this to end.

We left the motel and went to the Cowboy Museum. It was as nice as I remembered it. We had a great time. Candy got a lot of pictures, mostly of me. We were dressed like a cowboy and cowgirl. We fit right in, me with my long hair, hat and boots and Candy with her boots, great legs and hat. The statues and art work were pure. We felt right at home. When we left we drove through the rest of Oklahoma, through Arkansas and found a motel in Memphis, Tennessee.

The night was magical. Candy was in a comical mood, such a joy to be with.

At Nashville we found the Elvis Graceland and spent a day there. We toured his plane, his home and his stable and gravesite where he was buried. We both found it very interesting.

After we did the Elvis thing, we left Memphis, Tennessee, traveling north to Lexington, Kentucky when we came upon a Corvette Museum. Candy wanted to stop, so we did. They had a Corvette from each year that they were made. It was quite interesting. Years later, I heard the ground opened up under the museum and a number of the Corvettes were lost.

We arrived late in the evening, tired and hungry. We found a nice diner and a motel in the Lexington area. Daniel Boone is buried there and Lincoln's Homestead is close by, nice to know, but our main interest is the Kentucky Horse Parkland and the race track at Keeneland where they auction off the most famous thoroughbred race horses. Many of the very best stud horses have been bred on farms nearby.

The next morning we toured Keeneland Race Track inside out. We had breakfast with the jockeys, owners and trainers, many that we recognized from watching all the big races on TV. We both follow all the Triple Crown races, etc. We also saw some of the most beautiful horse flesh we've ever seen before. We watched a couple of races, did not bet and headed for the Kentucky Horse Park before it got too late. At the horse park we saw many statues of the most famous horses such as Man of War, Secretariat, etc. We were actually able to see and even pet a retired gelding named John Henry, who when purchased, cost his new owners a fortune and when raced, he never won. The owners decided he was a complete waste of money and they gelded him because his bad behavior made him dangerous to handle. From that time forward he never lost a race. The lesson learned was once you get your mind off of the ladies, you can settle down and win, but the owners who gelded him lost a fortune in breeding fees which would have far outweighed his track winnings. Why Secretariat is known as the greatest ever race horse was discovered after he died. He had a heart twice as big as any other horse.

As horse owner/lovers and outdoor people, this whole trip was a dream come true. Sharing this with Candy, who is so compatible and was such a pleasure to be with. After we left Kentucky we were nearing the end of our journey with a few days of vacation left. Candy didn't want it to ever end. I said the only thing we could do with the remaining few days is to end it with a bang in the biggest city of them all. We headed toward New York City. Times Square, Madam Tussauds Wax Museum, a Broadway show and a good meal atTavern on the Green, a romantic horse carriage ride through Central Park, and overnight stay in the Biltmore Hotel, crowned off our trip. We were ready for the final ride home. In a couple of hours we were in familiar territory but not eager to go back to our regular routines.

We were pleased to be greeted by our animals and pleased that my daughter had apparently done a good job with them in my absence. Candy seemed happy with the care her horse got at the stable where he was boarded.

Our office was moved from Kingston to Wilkes-Barre, Pennsylvania. I was more involved in cases at Wilkes-Barres; Court House. Now I saw a lot of Candy's sweet face.

In the meantime, my second daughter in North Dakota wanted to come home. I drove out, rented a trailer and brought her, my granddaughter, a big collie dog, their clothing, various furniture items, etc. home and moved them in with me.

Back at work I attended a class on wire-tapping given to our agents by the Drug Enforcement Association (DEA). - Everyone agreed this was a good tool but we also knew that the rules had to be followed closely or we could lose this valuable tool. If it was used to violate peoples' rights it would be taken away.

We ran several investigations using wire-tap We were very careful to insure no one's rights were tampered with and they resulted in many people being arrested and good seizures of vehicles and properties because they were used in the sales or delivery of illicit drugs.

We were asked by the District Attorney from another county to help them with a wire-tap investigation they were conducting. Several of our Agents went as observers and realized that the people conducting the wire-tap were violating the rights of persons being tapped. It seemed as though none of their people had any training and a report indicating our findings was given to our superiors.

We were told not to take part in the investigation. But after the investigation was over, we were instructed to participate in the drug raid that this same District Attorney was staging. A District Attorney who happened to be in the running for the job of Attorney General in the State of Pennsylvania. Agents, (undercover), from all over the State of Pennsylvania, checked into hotels in the area and moved under cover of darkness to the staging area, an abandoned super market to be met by scores of cameras and reporters. The aforementioned District Attorney gave the reporters an interview and we agents were given our assignments, targets to be arrested. I had one of the major targets whose family informed me that he was at the shore. He expected to be arrested yesterday. According to them, an article in the newspaper alerted everyone about the drug raid that was taking place now. When I reported back to the staging area, I was told all of the targets were telling the same story. Not to worry about it, my target would be picked up later.

I had been investigating a doctor in the aforementioned District Attorney's county and as I always did, I took my well prepared case and offered it to him (DA) for prosecution. He told me he could not prosecute that case because he and the doctor lived in the same housing area. He referred to my undercover works as being barbaric!

I called our headquarters in Harrisburg and one of our attorneys told me he reviewed the case. It looked good to him but no one in that office would prosecute it because the aforementioned DA would likely be elected as Attorney General. I gave the case to DEA for whatever action they deemed necessary. I heard later that they took action without any further assistance from me. They took the doctor's license, and he retired to Florida.

Another case I was working on in this same county involved two brothers, a dentist and a pharmacist. It involved State Police and DEA Agents. The dentist was a campaign manager for my new boss, the Attorney General who ran a successful campaign and was elected. The Regional Director I worked for was fired. The new Attorney General replaced him with one of his old Assistant District Attorneys' and a new Regional Director, a Corporal from the State Police who assisted him with his campaign, was hired as the new Regional Director. Neither knew beans about running an undercover organization. I started getting phone calls from people I was involved with in a criminal case. They would call the office looking for me so anyone he or she spoke to in the office just looked up on the wall, got my home phone number and gave it to them I questioned why my home phone number was up on the wall in the secretary's office. The new Regional Director whose idea it was to put our home phone numbers on the wall said when he wanted one of us he didn't want to have a hard time looking for our numbers.

It was clear that the Attorney and PSP Corporal were put there to direct our investigations in the direction that the Attorney General wanted them to go in.

Other instances of incompetence were like when State Police (PSP) informed me that a pharmacist was providing all the junkies with syringes without a prescription. I investigated and found that it was true. I contacted the office concerned with Medical Licensing and told them I had a problem with proving the pharmacist intended to or knowingly broke the law. I thought he might be doing it thinking he was helping junkies by preventing infection, etc. He certainly wasn't going to get rich giving syringes away. Both the Licensing Board and I thought it was a case that would better be handled by them. My new boss, the Corporal, took the case to the attorney and I was called into the office and informed that I must make the arrest of the pharmacist. After informing them of my reasons for not making an arrest, I was given a direct order to arrest. I arrested the pharmacist. The arrest was reported in the newspaper. Turns out the pharmacist was well-known.

A preliminary hearing was scheduled by the District Magistrate. As I suspected, he threw out the charges because his intent to commit a crime could not be proven.

This was also reported that I was ordered to make the arrest. When I got back to the office, the attorney and my boss, the Corporal, tried to ream my ass out, but failed. They tried to tell me not to ever use their name in a criminal complaint. I told them without their order to arrest, I had no probable cause to arrest, something which is always necessary.

Faced with their incompetence, I was questioning if I should try to transfer out of this office.

I was working on my case involving the pharmacist/dentist brothers. The dentist was the Attorney General's Campaign Manager. I started asking for assistance from DEA and they began sending one of their agents with me on this investigation. I learned that my Bureau Director was also related to the dentist, Campaign Manager and his brother, the pharmacist. Considering the facts in this case, I was beginning to feel quite intimidated. Every step I took was more provocative to persons in high places. He agreed and I proceeded with that investigation. The pharmacy, a store and restaurant, were seized in the hill section near a college with underground parking.

During this investigation it was learned that they were a large Islamic family and a member of that family was appointed by my new boss, the former District Attorney from that same county as the Bureau of Drug Control Director. The head of the State Police assigned to our region approached me and asked for help to conduct a highly secret investigation of a pharmacy and a pharmacist. He would not give me any information and as such I was limited as to how much help I could provide him. I later learned why he was being so secretive. His investigation, which he would normally turn over to me, was concerning our newly elected Attorney General and his dentist campaign manager's brother, the pharmacist all of whom were close friends. They ended up arresting the pharmacist on a minor charge, took him to the Magistrate where he paid a small bail, left and went right back and opened his pharmacy with illegal business as usual.

Had I conducted this investigation, the pharmacist would have lost his Pharmacist License, his Pharmacy License compliments of the Pennsylvania Board of Licensing and his DEA Registration, compliments of DEA.

Because of the high profile investigations status and because my bosses figured prominently, my involvement put me in a very provocative or dangerous position. Again, I requested assistance from DEA. Attorney

Rick Sponseller, a Federal Attorney from DEA and the Federal Marshal's Office from my old outfit when I served as a Sky Marshal, they came to my assistance. I began looking at and examining the pharmacy records and learned that the dentist has written a lot of prescriptions for patients for drugs not normally prescribed for by dentists, which is illegal.

The pharmacy was forfeited to the government. Because it was so well suited in the hill section on a main street, on a corner location in the city's college area, the pharmacy became a sub-station for law enforcement.

When my boss, our Attorney General, was imprisoned by Federal Attorneys on unrelated charges, I was energized because I felt there were a lot of questions in the investigations I began that were not answered to my satisfaction because I was transferred to avoid any provocative interference. I began looking for answers to my questions by re-opening those investigations involving the imprisoned Attorney General and his Campaign Manager, the dentist and his brother, the pharmacist who conspired to break drug laws in Pennsylvania and to get an attorney elected first as Attorney General and later to further his election as Governor of Pennsylvania. When headquarters learned of my intentions, I immediately

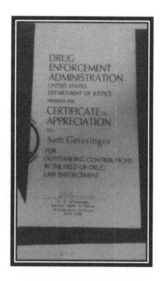

received a written order from the Attorney General designated to replace my imprisoned Attorney General, to consider that investigation closed. He then ran a successful campaign for Governor of Pennsylvania. He served one term as Governor.

While serving in the U.S. Air Force, my family and I lived among, and I had worked with various Muslims and Narcotics Agents while stationed in Turkey. I was also on the front lines as an original Sky Marshal in our fight against the Islamic Extremist Terrorists who were hijacking our most valuable commercial aircraft along with passengers and crew. Having served over twenty years as a member of the U.S. Air Force and over twenty-five years as a member of the Pennsylvania Office of Attorney General, I never disobeyed a lawful order. So I'll go to my grave with the big question unanswered: What purpose was served by Islamic members of that community who found it necessary to have the Attorney General and/or Governor of Pennsylvania in their back pocket?

Candy bought a new car and a new house where she could live rent free. I felt that this was a good time to break it off with her because I was still convinced the age difference could not work. Our times together were magic. We had more in common than ever but my children would never accept a woman I had in my life that was younger than they were.

Candy begged me but she soon came to believe me. Candy began dating a married man that couldn't stand horses. They dated for a short time. She wanted to get ready for a horse show. She and her boyfriend went to a horse supply store where they had to cross railroad tracks. Before they left the store, they were seen and heard to be arguing. When they left the store, her boyfriend drove her car into a train and Candy was killed instantly, her chest being crushed. Her boyfriend did not sustain any injuries. This accident happened shortly after Candy lost her beloved Father.

At the funeral, Candy's Mother told me that Candy would still be alive if I hadn't left her. I met her boyfriend who tried to tell me about her feelings for me but I told him to leave me alone. I felt so bad. God bless her. At the funeral I couldn't believe that someone so vibrant, so talented and so young, was no longer with us.

Betty was at the funeral and she told me the owner at the stable was trying to steal Candy's horse from Candy's Mother by not selling the horse for her. I told Candy's Mother that I would take Candy's horse to Wilson College and I would sell it. The owner was not going to have Candy's horse because her Mother couldn't pay for the board. When I went to pick up Candy's horse the stable owner said she found a buyer for the horse. Candy's Mother was very happy with the money she got for the horse.

My heart was broken. Tears kept flowing. I thank God that Candy and I took that long trip together. Candy and I saw **OUR** America, more importantly, America got to meet Candy. She brought joy to everyone she met. What a glorious person. Honey, I'll never forget you. Maybe we'll meet in heaven and finally have that life together. +God Wink!

I began making an effort to find women who were at least within ten years of my age. The first one was Becky who worked in a photo shop. She would receive my film, have it developed, and return the film and pictures to me. She was overly friendly, seemed very interested, and from our conversations, it was obvious that she had taken a lot of interest in the pictures she had developed for me. I started checking her out and found out she was divorced with two children, a boy and a girl. Becky was blonde, tall and slender with a nice body, approximately thirty-five years of age. I asked her to meet me at a local hotel for dinner and she agreed. We had a nice dinner and after drinking and dancing, she appeared anxious to join me in my room. She became more attractive as the night went on. When she took her clothes off, she could see how eager I was also. She was very light and the more I lifted her, the more amorous she became. The night was magic. It seemed I spent the whole night inside of her. She said she never had a man manhandle her the way I did. It really turned her on.

As time went on, I became more and more lonely after Candy's untimely death. The more I thought about her, the more I thought that I made the biggest mistake of my life. Candy did everything she could to ensure that our life together would be one of complete compatibility, something I obviously didn't have with my own wife. The Mother of my children, my ex-wife, abandoned our children. She didn't attend the second wedding of either of our oldest and second oldest daughter, not the wedding of my youngest daughter. She discouraged visits from our children.

I put in for a transfer to Region 1. I realized that if I kept provoking everyone I worked for by insisting on following all the leads no matter where they went or who they involved, I'd get killed, fired or arrested on some trumped up charge. My bodyguard, The DEA Agent, and I were following leads in this case checking out the dentist's prescriptions found in the pharmacy, for drugs not normally prescribed for their dental patients. We were invited and entered the home of a feisty older woman who admitted she was related to everyone, that she did get the referred to prescription from the dentist and filled the prescription at her nephew's pharmacy. She also informed us that she was a good friend of my boss, the Attorney General.

When my bodyguard, the DEA Agent and I left her home, as soon as our feet hit the side walk, we both said it at the same time, "I can hear the phones ringing now"!

The DEA Agent left for his home. I went back to my office to face the music. As soon as I entered I was told to report to the Attorney's Office. In I went, faced with the Attorney and the Corporal who screamed, asking what was I doing in that woman's home. My answer was simple. We were following leads in my case. I left them stammering and went home. I had a good day. When I got home, my boss, the Bureau Director, was on my phone apologizing for overlooking my request for transfer. He told me that my transfer was effective the very next Monday.

We experienced the same scenario at another drug raid in Williamsport, Pennsylvania. My team was assigned a target. We left the staging area, arrived at the designated apartment and effected the arrest of the perpetrator. He was under our control when we heard people arriving at the perpetrator's door, perhaps customers with intentions of making a drug purchase. We hid waiting for their arrival intending to make additional unplanned arrests as necessary. Unknown to us was the fact that a mistake had been made back at the staging area and a second team was given the same target we had. Because it was not closed properly, when they knocked on the apartment door it swung open enough to see men inside with guns. They began shooting and wounded a Williamsport police team member from my team. I recognized the team member from our bureau and ordered our team to stand down. Both of our team leaders made a report immediately. I felt assured that my report was accurate and I returned to my normal duty.

I took the perpetrator to the Magistrate. He didn't make bail and I deposited him in jail. Correcting the mistakes made at the staging area was not my concern.

I reported to my new Region 1 as required. I spoke to my new Regional Director, a female whom I knew since the beginning of my bureau employment, one I had respect for knowing her job. She expected good case work from me, she knew my reputation. I didn't like leaving my old cases which were very high profile cases, not just cases that involved persons associated with our boss, the Attorney General and my Bureau

Director, but also a doctor who had been involved with a handsome young man. Although he was now of age, the doctor, according to the young man's parents, had maintained his addiction, took him on vacation to Florida, and controlled his very life for the doctor's own sexual satisfaction. The last evidence that needed further investigation was a report I had that the doctor and his young man rolled out of the doctor's car in the parking lot at a McDonald's Restaurant. The doctor was performing CPR on the young man who was bare from the waist down. The doctor asked someone to call an ambulance. It was reported that in spite of the fact that the hospital had an efficient emergency room staff on duty when the doctor and his patient arrived, the doctor insisted that only he be permitted to attend to his patient. The doctor, although he said it was not a drug overdose, administered "Narcan" to his patient and he survived.

-

In my new region, I got involved with cases, wire taps, seizures of money earned selling illegal drugs, automobiles and properties used in the manufacture, use, or purchased with proceeds of illegal drug sales and interdiction. We began training local police on procedures to cut down on the quantities of drugs being brought into their cities, towns, boroughs, and rural areas, at their bus, train and air terminals.

State law requires that doctors or pharmacists who dispense controlled substances must make a report to DEA and our Regional Officers monthly. The monitoring of these reports also provide many leads and many cases are initiated as a result.

False reports by a pharmacist to cover his own drug use, resulted in the loss of his license and the loss of his pharmacy license and eventually his facility.

When the U.S. Attorney's Office conducted their own investigation of our boss, he was already campaigning for Governor of Pennsylvania. He was allowed to plead guilty to a lesser offense and he was sentenced to spend thirteen months in a Federal Prison. He lost his license to practice law. Another Attorney was appointed to serve the remaining term of the convicted Attorney General and I began to get questions about my old cases, why they were never closed. It seemed those persons the Attorney, (ex- DA), Regional Director, (ex-PSP Corporal), never assigned an agent to persue my old cases.

I started an investigation concerning the incompetence of my old bosses. I received a letter from the new Pennsylvania Attorney General ordering me to consider the whole case closed.

Currently a female attorney from the same location of the crooked Attorney General was elected as Pennsylvania's new Attorney General. One of her first duties was to fire the Regional Director in the region she came from, just as the crooked one did. As of now, she has been convicted of crimes committed by her as Pennsylvania's first female Attorney General. No sentence as yet!

Meanwhile when Becky learned that I only occupied my hotel room for a short time before a drug raid, she suggested that we not let the room go to waste.

I wouldn't join her in her apartment because of the presence of her children. I agree my room should not be wasted.

Becky joined me in my hotel room. Because there was a nice warm pool, I told her to bring her swimsuit. When she arrived I was in my swimming suit. She immediately went into the bathroom and put her suit on. When she came out with her bikini on, we went to the pool and entered it. Just as it began getting dark and there was little lighting, I started reaching for her bikini. I just wanted enough room to enter her. She was so comfortable in the water but stopped me, saying that the life guard was watching us, he knows what we're doing. I asked if his watching wouldn't make it more exciting. She didn't answer me, she just stopped resisting. Now the lifeguard was really interested! We finished it back in our room, but the excitement was still there. I can only tell you that our room was not wasted!

I was developing a case. I was informed that persons in the legal and medical professions were passing an attractive woman around among the professionals and that they were all using her to satisfy their sexual desires. This was going on in the same district that our crooked Attorney General came from. It had progressed to such a point that many of the participants were getting very nervous. It all started with the subject (attractive woman) seeking to help her jailed husband and went to the first attorney who learned that she had a serious drug habit. Attorney number one had a doctor friend who had a prescription pad and a pen. After a while, this same doctor complained that he would get in trouble for prescribing all those narcotics until the female subject agreed to perform for doctor number one. Needless to say, no arrests were made and deals were being made all over when they learned **The Provocative Barbarian** was on the case.

Drug raids were particularly dangerous because we never knew the people we had to arrest. We were not always familiar with the targets to be arrested and we were not familiar with the local people we were assigned to work with. For example, when I first graduated from the Academy, the older agents had been conducting investigations and they had to rely on the graduating class to conduct raids all over the state, targets whose investigations were complete except for their arrest. All I did for the first six months was make arrests.

One arrest in particular stands out in my memory. It was common practice to check into a hotel or motel the night before a scheduled drug raid. In the middle of the night we would move into a staging area to be assigned to a local police team to lead the team into the target's area to make the arrest. Most of the time you did not know the local police. You did not know the local police, you did not know what experience they had. For example, this one officer grabbed a man, not yet identified, at the door, put him and his shotgun against the wall. I was able to secure the shotgun before the man being searched was able to grab it. The first local policeman to reach the bottom of the stairs inside the house was killed by the main target standing at the top of the stairs in his underwear. The shooter was easily controlled and arrested as soon as he realized to resist would only end up with his demise. +God Wink!

The same scenario in a Philadelphia drug raid brought me into the bedroom of the target in bed nude with his nude girlfriend. When I awakened them and advised him as to our purpose for being there, he began to reach for his pants laying on a chair next to the bed. I stopped him, indicating that I would give him what he would use to get dressed. When I picked up those same pants, a loaded .45 caliber hand gun was revealed. +God Wink!

Another case I developed was working with a female informant provided by the District Attorney. She was promised a lesser sentence by the court if she assisted us in our investigations. The informant told us that she had been getting narcotics from a Muslim doctor who it appears was breaking every rule in the book.

We had to work with one of our female agents because our informant had to be strip searched before we sent her in and immediately after she returned to us. This is done to keep her honest and insure her integrity if her testimony would be needed in court. We wired her up and taped her visit with the doctor. He gave her narcotics of different strengths in the same unlabeled container to assist her with her addiction. He gave her Muslim literature to persuade her to change religions.

From that first visit to the doctor I knew what I needed to know about the doctor so that I could cut out the informant and make the buys myself. A few days later I went in undercover and persuaded the doctor to assist me with my addiction. He gave me varied strengths of narcotics in an unlabeled test tube vial, all of which are illegal. An arrest was made. An Attorney from our office prosecuted the case. Through the preliminary hearing it went before the DA and he made a deal through the doctor's attorney. The doctor pled guilty to a misdemeanor.

Becky and I traveled to Columbus, Ohio where every year they produce one of our country's biggest week-long horse shows. We also traveled to Toronto, Canada where another big-time horse show was held. We stayed in the nicest Holiday Inn that I've ever encountered. It was one of the tallest buildings in Toronto. The top floor restaurant revolved. The food was excellent and the atmosphere was out of this world. In both cases, Becky enjoyed the hotels more than any horse activity. Becky took one horseback riding lesson and then quit. We decided to take our children to Disneyland in Florida jointly. After we arrived at our hotel my youngest daughter took a disliking to Becky and threw her in the motel pool with all her clothes on. That put a damper on my relationship with Becky. We just could not get going in the same direction. The sex was the only thing Becky and I didn't have any problem with. We got naked in the back seat of my car, to the rear of a drive-in movie. We discovered that billboards provided parking spaces behind them for secret or private meetings. All of these places added something to each of our sexual encounter. The fear that we might be discovered seemed to enliven each encounter. To this day each time I travel the same highways and spot a familiar billboard, I tingle a little bit remembering what went on there. I knew that after Becky got thrown into the pool at the hotel we had to dump the kids because we all shared one room. Becky and I ran like two children through the halls of the motel. Using darkness as cover, we entered my car and had hot sex on the front passenger seat. It was great and seemed to soothe us both a lot. The next day we were all in my car driving to Sea World and there it was. As we climbed a hill and the sun shined on the windshield, two beautiful foot prints of Becky's became visible. We had to do some quick thinking until those footprints were wiped clean. Becky explained apologetically saying how did I expect her to get her thrust otherwise?

About five years ago, I was working undercover to purchase larger quantities of narcotics. The critters I was working on couldn't provide the quantity that I wanted. I knew this going in. That's how I would pyramid the investigation, to get introduced to the bigger dealers. My office provided me with a number of cover cars for protection, important because I didn't know where the contacts would be taking me to make the drug purchases. Two of my contacts were in the front seat of their car and one of my contacts sat with me in the back seat. The guy sitting with me was making me nervous because he was scraping his veins in his arm with a big hunting knife, complaining that he had to get a new set of works. I knew what he meant. His tolerance had increased to the point where he had a need of a larger needle to push larger quantities into his body in order to get the high his body needed and wanted. He knew the person I was to meet could take care of all his needs. They drove me from Allentown into New Jersey, then into New York City. I was to meet their dealer and make the purchase in the restroom of a restaurant. I spotted on of our cover cars and felt confident they were doing their job taking pictures and good notes in order to put everything down in our reports and arrest warrants for the prosecution of the persons involved. Once in the restroom, I passed out. I woke up in a New York City Hospital. I was told I had bleeding ulcers. I didn't realize I had this problem because the Vagus Nerves in my stomach were cut while I was in Turkey, leaving me with no ability to feel pain or understand the blood loss. My cover was responsible for locating me after the dealer left me there minus my drugs and my buy money. I was transferred to a hospital in Kingston, Pennsylvania where I recovered and I was later able to testify in New York City to put my contacts and their dealer in jail. Thank God for good cover. +God Wink!

I had heard the rumors in our church about our married minister with children being seen in compromising positions with a young, recently divorced woman with adult children. I knew her and she knew of me and my divorce status. She began showing me attention one day after church in a restaurant that we were both eating in, she with her adult children and me with friends. I decided to see where she wanted to go with this. We made a date to meet for dinner in a hotel.

On the night that we met, she admitted that the rumors were true but she said she wanted to stop it. She had been lonely living alone. After we ate she offered to take me to her apartment. I didn't think I could damage her reputation any further being from a small town and I thought if the

Minister learned she was dating a divorced man from his church, he would back off and settle back in with his family and the church.

Once we were in her apartment, she provided us with drinks. We sat on her couch and almost immediately she decided to impress me wither oral sex skills. I was quite impressed, even more so with her body and her bedroom activities. A few times she visited me at my home which was more private. I knew she was still making contact with the minister because she was often deep in thought. After a few weeks she and the minister disappeared. I felt that he must have offered to divorce his wife and marry her. That was easy. I wasn't planning to take that any further anyway.

Filled with disdain for myself because of the turn my life had taken, I decided to get serious about finding someone to settle down with. I gave up on the compatible companion thing. I was convinced that there was no one out there now that Candy was gone.

I started taking an interest in another beauty from my church who was distinguished and dignified. I didn't want to rush her so I didn't do the obvious. I didn't approach her at church. I learned from conducting my own investigation that her names was Ester. She was divorced one time, had no children and owned a nice home in the gated community of Lake Hauto. The lake was great for boating, fishing and swimming. Tennis and basketball courts were also available for our use. I considered her to be a good candidate. I learned that she had a close relationship with her sister who had a family and lived in a home behind hers. Both sisters came from Germany and Ester's sister sold fish from a booth at a very popular weekly auction in Hometown where they spent a lot of time together keeping each other company. I started buying fish from her sister and making conversation much as I would if I was trying to work my way in to make a drug purchase undercover. I was happy to learn that they did not sell drugs, just good fish. Many weeks later we started dating. We joined each other at church. She had a big dog named Duke which suited me as I had several dogs of my own. We visited each other's homes. We boated, fished, swam, and played tennis but she would not ride the horses with me. A year later we got married. She didn't want a big wedding so we had a small ceremony in our church conducted by a new minister. She moved into my home. My youngest daughter was close to graduating from college. I bought her a small second-hand sporty two-seater Honda for graduation and I hid it in Ester's garage so my daughter would be surprised when she received it. My daughter graduated from college.

In order to make a long story short, the marriage only lasted five years. My three daughters and I were all very close. Ester had no children and was either jealous or resentful of my close loving relationship with my children. I told her she should sell her home or I should sell mine because it was ridiculous supporting two homes, recreational fees, street cleaning, taxes and repairs when we only lived in one.

Being unfamiliar with undercover procedures, my new boss gave my home phone number to a confidential female informant who kept calling my house, annoying my wife. She would not listen to reason so I told her I wanted a divorce. I gave her five thousand dollars to cover her moving expenses. It was done, no more claim on me.

To pay attention to the type of drugs involved with the persons to be arrested is one thing that you learn very quickly while making arrests in drug law enforcement. Persons on narcotics are more easily handled. The word itself means to be numb. It's that state of numbness that the addict seeks, a state of mind when you are not awake and not asleep. Think of a scene such as this: A narcotics addict sitting on a park bench high on narcotics watching young men or women playing basketball. The addict, slouching and wasting his life away in a destructive lifestyle, thinking those persons engaged in a healthy lifestyle playing basketball, don't know where it's at!

Persons on stimulants, (speed), are a different person altogether. Think of those persons addicted to speed going to the shore for a weekend to party. Addicted to speed, they can party all day and all night without need for sleep, until they're on the way home from the shore and their car crosses over to the other side of the highway. Literally they crashed, killing a whole family with children heading for the shore. Speed allows an addict to push their bodies to their extreme and when they crash there is no telling what they may do. Often hallucinating, (imaginary perceptions), they sometimes kill, imagining someone wants to kill them.

I had an arrest warrant for a speed freak from Bradford County. I went to the courthouse looking for assistance because I had nothing to do with this case development and I was unfamiliar with the area. The Sheriff volunteered to go with me as he knew the area and was familiar with the person to be arrested, he was a repeat offender.

We traveled together to the home of the person identified on the warrant. We went to the front door of his home where an older woman answered the door, identifying herself as the addict's mother. She told us that her son was working on an old automobile to the rear of their home. We thanked her and located him as indicated, all covered in mud and grease. As we were identifying ourselves, he exploded and the Sheriff grabbed him as he was trying to escape. The Sheriff received an elbow to his nose which rendered him unconscious. On my own, I still had an order to arrest this young man so I grabbed him. I didn't remember how it happened, but the next thing I remembered was the addict in cuffs. He was face down in the mud. I was on top of him with my knee in the back of his neck. His mother was trying to pull me off of him. I called an ambulance which quickly arrived. They said he was ok. They took the unconscious Sheriff to a nearby hospital. I read the prisoner his rights, advised him of his charges and took him to a Magistrate who ordered heavy bail which he couldn't pay. I was thrilled to deposit him in jail so I could get my messy ass and car home to get cleaned up.

I tried to figure it all out. After all these years, I can only guess that good training automatically kicked in and I did what was necessary to get the job done. I checked on the Sheriff who had a busted nose but was ok otherwise. I thanked him, wished him well and said good-bye.

Some of the most interesting characters I've ever met while working in Narcotics were Scags and Bags. Scags rode a motorcycle and Bags was his girl. Scags into a little trouble and the District Attorney offered them a break if they would work with us to investigate else, beautiful, well-endowed and educated.

We rented an apartment for them in a nearby city and covered them while they became established with the local gangs. They were doing well until one of the gang members took a liking to Scag's motorcycle and stole it. Scags did the unthinkable. He went to the police and blew their cover. The police got his motorcycle back, something we could have done without blowing their cover. I was instructed to go to their apartment and move them out of there. Their lives were in grave danger. Scags was considered a definite hazard. The Bureau got rid of him but Bags was educated and considered a valuable asset. She was enrolled and attended our Academy at Wilson College where I taught several classes.

Bags and I became quite close but for her own safety, upon graduation, she was assigned to regions on the other side of the state.

I would see her occasionally now and again when agents gathered from all over the state for a drug raid or sometime during various training sessions. Bags was popular and was always connected to one agent or another.

At sixty-five years of age, I was reaching retirement age and had over twenty-five years on the job. My senses weren't what they used to be. I didn't wish to be detrimental to fellow agents. I was supervising what everyone knew was my last case. Because I was using female confidential informants, I required a female agent to assist searching and covering the informants. Bags was assigned for those reasons. What a surprise! Bags told me she requested the assignment as she wanted to work with me for the last time. The female informants were gay and they were to meet a doctor in a gay bar to make a large purchase of narcotics. They needed a lot of cover because of the location and nature of the bar. We had about twelve agents covering plus Bags and myself.

As was our practice and because it was my last case before retirement, we all met in a secluded bar. I bought a round of drinks for all agents and two informants while discussing our individual part in the investigation and getting it all down on my final report. As each informant told us how it went down for them, we were all pleased that it appeared this was a good case. As each agent related their specific part, we were pretty high knowing the subject doctor was dead in the water. I was well pleased with everyone assigned to this case. As professional an operation as I ever witnessed. As the informants and each agent departed, I began to realize Bags didn't have the usual agent hanging in there. When I asked her about it she told me she was going home with me. She wanted something to remember me by. When we arrived at my home I was really high on Bags. She snuggled all the way home, massaging my body as I drove. It was very tantalizing. Upon our arrival, I apologized because I had just purchased a new bedroom suit and I hadn't finished putting it together yet. She said she didn't mind using the other bedroom but first she wanted to shower. We both showered. There were two showers, why not? I slipped into some patriotic bikini shorts. When we first met she was already under the covers in the spare bedroom. As I reached for her she threw the covers aside and I witnessed the most beautiful body I had ever seen. I told her she was a dream come true. She said she often thought of me and she said that she never did feel that she properly thanked me for getting her out of a tight spot when her cover was blown. We melted into each other's embrace, two old friends, me doing everything possible to insure that she would enjoy out last time together. The next morning we found our clothes where we left them in the showers.

After we showered again I caught her taking my picture while I was trying to get into my pants. I asked her what she was doing. She simply said, "I told you I wanted to have something to remember you by." I then drove her back to the bar to pick up her state car. We hugged and kissed I thought sadly, for the last time.

On the day scheduled for my retirement party, I arrived at the office in my own car because when I turned in my state-owned automobile, one of my friends drove me home.

The Conference Room was always designated as the room where we all had our retirement parties. When I entered the Conference Room, I was faced with a big fancy cake, many gifts, a plaque from the newly assigned Attorney General when the crooked Attorney General went to prison. It was the actual badge, number 178, that I carried from 7-11-73 to 1-9-98 and my Commonwealth of Pennsylvania Office of Attorney General identification card with my picture and signature attesting to the fact that I was a duly appointed Narcotics Agent. It was a real surprise because I had to surrender it along with my gun when I gave notice of my retirement. I also received my .38 caliber stainless steel S&W revolver, along with a plaque from the Pennsylvania Attorney General in appreciation for my service. I also received a leather-bound letter of appreciation of service from the Governor and House of Representatives. Something I didn't notice at first was a picture of me trying to get into my pants with my patriotic underwear on display. I looked for bags and when our eyes met, she said, "Gotcha! How was my undercover work "Teach". I took that picture off of the bulletin board and until this day I treasure that picture more than anything else I received on the day of my third retirement.

Retirement is such a healthy thing for my organization to got through. It opens up new or better positions for new and let's face it, better employees.

After Democrats just received the worst beating at the poles beaten by Donald Trump, I just learned that Nancy Pelosi, after serving two terms

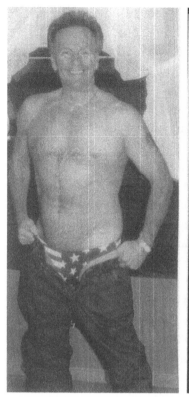
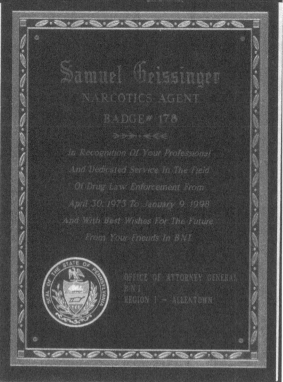

as Majority Whip, and Joe Biden, two terms as Vice-President to President Obama's failed Presidential run of eight years. Nancy was famous for advising her Majority of Democratic Representatives and good old Joe went along with her advice to not read the bill on Obama Healthcare, sign it first, then you can read it. Biden just announced that he will probably run for President in 2020 and Nancy Pelosi just won another term, this time as Minority Whip. Some people just never want to relinquish power even when they know there are better, stronger, and younger people more qualified waiting in the wings of that organization. I could have tried to stay on the job longer myself, convincing myself that at sixty-five I would be just as I was in my youth, more able to run six flights of stairs if necessary and take out someone threatening the life or lives of one or more of my co-workers. As in cards, the song says, "Ya gotta know when to fold 'em".

CHAPTER 5

Retirement

My life seemed to stop upon retirement, January 9, 1998. What does one do at age sixty-five when you still feel strong and viral, unmarried with an empty nest, horses and dogs, but no wife and no children. One of my daughters' lived close-by in Tamaqua but was completely engaged with a husband and two step children. What with work on weekdays and a campsite where there wasn't any telephone service on weekends and holidays and my youngest daughter married and living a happy life with horses and dogs on a farm in Iowa. I began stopping at a nearby golf course for meals and human company. I noticed Nina, a beautiful young, Italian woman who seemed very timid, shy and obviously a little frightened. I learned that she was raising her own family with seven children. We began to talk the stories she told me were funny to listen to, but horrifying to her. I told her she should write a book about those amusing stories. One of those stories was about the children who were jumping out of a second story window onto a snow pile put next to her home by a snow plow crew. Tired from working a tough job as a waitress at a busy golf club, she was trying to get some rest when a woman watching her children jumping out the window, knocked on her door. She told another story about bringing all the TV's and telephones to work with her so the children would go to school and how the children devised a way to plug a phone borrowed from one of their friends' into the jack installed on the outside of their house. Then there was the time she called me to say one of her children was missing. I picked her up and we located her missing child who spent the night in a hospital. Many of the returning soldiers suffered greatly from post-traumatic stress disorder and had a truly hard time returning to life as they knew it. Nina understood this and was considerate. She did everything she could to keep her children together and safe because she was needed by them. She had to begin riding her bike to work. She couldn't use the old van anymore and eventually she had to junk it. Between those times when I helped her, we began riding our bikes for pleasure. I found a trail along the river that we both enjoyed. We could eat in a restaurant before making the return trip that we both enjoyed, aside from the occasional bear we encountered along the trail. We became best friends, almost too close. There were twenty-two years between us. There were times when I wanted to take our relationship further and times she said she wanted to, but we never did. We both decided to keep it dignified. She unselfishly shared her family and relatives with me. I felt like one of her family, being invited to all of their gatherings. They filled my empty nest.

Nina and I started going to Farm Shows, recreational parks, horse auctions, rodeos and many other excursions, too many to mention. The more I saw her, the closer, more compatible we became. My Father, Mother and all of my siblings were gone. I had an Aunt, Mother's youngest sister, and her husband, Uncle Mike, who lived for over one hundred years. When my Aunt died in her late eighties, my Uncle, who lived in a nursing home and legally blind, had no one. On her dying bed his wife begged me to care for him. He was a devoted Catholic and and an Italian. He and Nina loved each other. I had an old school chum who was a priest at Nina's church. Being disenchanted with my church, I began going to church with Nina every Sunday. Since I joined the Catholic Church, I felt that I should bring something to God as a sacrifice.

About Nina: She is so upfront and honest, it's almost criminal. She still exercises every day, is very healthy, has dark brown hair, fascinating blue eyes, tans early, slender with a small body and beautiful butt and legs. In 2008 I had open-heart surgery with six vein by-passes which curtailed any opportunity I had to ride my bike. In 2016 I had surgery for a cancerous tumor on my colon. The cancer moved to my liver. This again required another surgery and months of Chemo Infusion.

My vow before God, that much harder having experienced love or lust in the past with someone, (Candy), who was much too young for me. Considering how hard it must have been for Nina being left alone with seven young children, I felt she had enough troubles without me adding to them. She had fears of abandonment. She had fears for each of her children. Nina did not like entering a place full of people unless I took the lead. The thing that I admired most about her was her dedication to her children. I always stayed in the lives of my children and vowed that I always would. My wife abandoned her children so you might know why I admired Nina.

One of the things that she had a hard time with was how long it took her children to give birth to her grandchildren. She was getting older and she was getting very concerned. Her arms ached to feel her grandchildren. Nina's youngest son wrecked his automobile in Virginia. He wanted it home and Nina asked me if I knew how she could help him. I told her I could tow it home with my pick-up truck. How could I avoid it? This was her youngest son whom she called "Bud" just as my Mother nicknamed me "Bud". We were both born on New Year's Eve! While in Virginia, Nina received a phone call from her daughter. She had checked into a hospital in Binghamton, New York and had given birth to Nina's first grandchild, a "BOY! We towed Bud's car to her home and left immediately for the hospital. I witnessed Nina's joy when she held her first grandchild. I could see from the beginning that she was hooked. It was a joke from then on; I would ask Nina if she needed a fix, the answer always being YES!

Upon leaving the hospital in New York, her daughter, who was a trained nurse with a Master's Degree in Psychology, soon moved in with her new son while studying for her State board exams. Having them living with

A MIGHTY PROUD & BEAUTIFUL GRANDMOTHER

5 IT's A BOY ALEXANDER HOMYAK

her, helping them out at a time when they needed it most, was a blessing for everyone.

Nina, who was in the habit of taking long walks all over the valley was now pushing her grandson everywhere. In winter or summer, it didn't matter. Many of our local residents commented on her dedication. One of the best gifts I ever gave her was a trailer for the back of her bike. We could put her grandson in that trailer with a couple of toys and he'd be so content, never complaining, even if we rode together all day. We would place his car seat in the middle of the back seat of my pick-up truck and he went everywhere with us. He was never a problem and his Mother had help getting licensed and established as a Registered Nurse.

All of Nina's options were open. She had many boyfriends and through it all we remained good friends. I've loved her and always respected her friendship. After ten years of retirement in 2008, I had cataract surgery in my left eye and open heart surgery, (six by-passes). Ten years later, 2016, I had a colon tumor, (cancer) which had moved to my liver requiring surgery and six months of Chemo treatments every other week. I had a cataract removed from my right eye in 2017, and now have 20/20 eye sight and no sign of cancer. The prayers and support from my family, Nina, who was with me every step of the way, the prayers and support from her family and relatives, along with our church and its congregation all have helped in my recovery.

Nina's first grandson had a sister two years younger, named after Nina.

Nina's oldest daughter married and had a son. Another daughter married and has two daughters and a son. Her youngest son married, had a son and a daughter and her oldest son married and they are expecting their baby in October. Her two youngest daughters, unmarried and living in California are extremely successful in their careers. It's amazing, Nina is so pleased and so proud of the way her family turned out.

Nina's home is almost completely remodeled thanks to her and the help of her latest boyfriend who is extremely competent and willing to help with the labor. Just a few years ago she could never believe she would ever be capable of her accomplishments.

Our friendship remains strong and enjoyable throughout. We have been greatly encouraged in the midst of our troubles and sufferings, dear Nina, because you allowed me to remain strong in my faith.

If I had any success in my attempts to encourage Nina to write her story, I don't know. She has shown no obvious signs.

She has had some success by gifts of books over the years encouraging me to write a book inspired by true experiences in my life. Nina has taken it further by putting what I write into her computer and searches in her computer for any interesting stories relating to copy writing protection and or publishers.

Nina's current boyfriend is a nice man near her age, who has befriended her for approximately ten years, but still no talk about taking their relationship a step closer. What I like about him is he doesn't seem to have any problem with Nina and I doing things together: Church every Sunday, family gatherings, medical appointments, dining out, etc. I never spent a night in her home and she has never spent a night in my home. It never even occurred to either of us and that's what has kept our friendship so strong. Prior to joining her church and our relationship with my old school chum,

who's a priest, and my mentor, Uncle Mike, which we shared, I never would have thought a friendship like ours was possible. The things Nina and I share seem to be things her boyfriend has no interest in.

When I think about this friendship with Nina, I sum it up like this: We will never be lonely from the start of each day to its end if we walk life's pathway with love in our hearts, side by side with a friend.

Little Nina, as we refer to her, is like a shadow of her Grandmother Nina. I've never seen a Grandchild who instigates as much time to be spent with a Grandmother as she does. I've never seen so much love between a Grandmother and Grandchild. They bake and sew together. She loves going to church with us and shopping and enjoying a meal together. As I write this, the two Nina's are visiting a young daughter, who happens to be a Flight Attendant, sharing First Communion with her three Grandchildren in Houston, Texas.

This is the same daughter who honored Nina, her Mother, by asking her to walk her down the aisle when she got married. I was invited also. It was a very joyous occasion, a beautiful wedding with all the trimmings. As I learned while attending that wedding, Nina was ill and very distressed throughout the wedding but like the trooper she is, Nina never told anyone, not wanting to affect that happy occasion for all concerned.

I went with Nina who bought a gown for the aforementioned occasion. She and her daughter were beautiful walking down the aisle together in that very formal occasion in a beautiful church. Upon our arrival back

in Pennsylvania, there was a long period of recovery for Nina and many nurses' visits. I hoped I might help her recovery if I visited frequently and if I helped her improve her home. I did this by installing a new roof and I extended it out and installed a new porch. She could now sit on her new porch and enjoy the days ahead.

During my recovery to include five hours of chemo infusion every other Wednesday for two years, Nina took me for each visit and stayed with me for the duration. I observed other patients being dropped off or coming on their own. Nina kept her family and our church advised as to my progress. I can now say it was this and the tremendous support of my two daughters that helped me recover and my cancer is now in remission.

ANOTHER NOTE OF INTEREST:

My number two daughter from Tamaqua came to live with me. She had tests done and it was determined that she would have triple by-pass, open heart surgery. She and I are doing quite well, she's back at work now and we help each other with the chores, loving every minute of caring for our farm and its animals.

Nina's oldest son, the last of her children to be married so far, married a beautiful young woman from New York. My daughter and I were invited to the wedding celebration. This too was a wonderful wedding celebration. I had an opportunity to see all of Nina's children and relatives again. It was like old times. The last thing I heard about this affair was that Nina is looking forward to adding another grandchild to her gorgeous brood, results of this most recent marriage of her oldest son.

Nina is still in the process of improving her home. She is having the exterior completely remodeled as this is being written. She's had a cat for years but now she has a dog given to her by her oldest son and added chickens and another dog she rescued. The animals have added to her great pleasure at home. She still has two unmarried daughters who might possibly increase her family's size, much to her happiness. Her family is pretty spread out around the country but she travels often to visit them.

Nina's children are all doing well. We are proud of their achievements over the years, now to include those of her grandchildren. Nina has a lot to be proud of.

I only have two children left. I'm proud of my own accomplishments, proud that I have always been here for my children. I only helped one through college and marriage. The other two I helped in their marriages and provided them shelter when necessary. My farm has grown and it is beautiful. I own a horse who was born on the farm thirty-eight years ago. She's been blind in her right eye for several years and we give her medicine for worming and sore joints daily and special senior grain and soft hay because her teeth aren't what they used to be. We had her mother, a real good quarter horse on the farm, for over thirty years. Her stud was a real good race horse named Restless Wind. There was only one time that our horse herd reached nine and we've always had a lot of dogs who had free reign over the farm.

My oldest daughter died at age forty-eight from complications as a diabetic. She had four children. Losing a child is the worst thing that can happen to a parent.

Nina related a similar experience. She had twin boys and one died after birth. Likewise, my first wife lost our second child, a stillborn boy. Unlike Nina, I never had the opportunity to hold my boy in my arms or even look at him. Knowing Nina the way I do, she was heartbroken.

My second eldest daughter is still young, (fifties), and beautiful. She lives with me. We get along well, sharing the chores and helping each other. She works with children in a Tamaqua school and she has an active social life.

My youngest daughter is still married, living on a farm in Iowa. This is much to her liking because it's similar to the life she had here on our farm. Her husband has worked in Omaha, Nebraska as an engineer since leaving college. This daughter never had children.

I have a granddaughter and great granddaughter living in Florida. We haven't seen them since they moved from Kentucky to Florida because of my age and the distance between us.

Our farm gives us a lot of comfort. Maintenance is becoming more of a problem. I'll start looking for help with the chores. I don't ever want to leave. The air and water are the best. I have enough land to walk with the dogs or just roam on and the view is so satisfying. It's not unusual to see a fox, raccoon, rabbit, or squirrel, groundhog, coyote or deer families taking up residence on the farm because everything is here for them. There's a stream flowing from west to east, spring water filling a few small ponds with fish, turtles, frogs, ducks, crane, and heron. Ever since I've been here I've been building brush piles on the back of the property to provide shelter for them all. This pleases the Game Commission as well as the critters who live here.

I realize time must be getting short in more ways than one. As I've said many times in the past, I'm happier than a puppy with two tails. No matter how things go, I'm confident that I have a good relationship with my God who satisfies me.

1937 — AMANGE RAILWAY EXPRESS AGENT & TONY GUNDELMAN — MIDDLEWARD

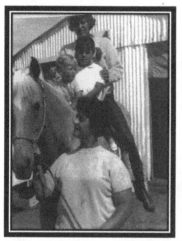

mother and dad

3rd place

Narc

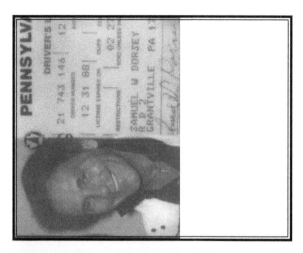

COGNAC

I WILL NEVER TELL

The Wawona Tree - 26 feet through opening
Yosemite Nat'l

CPSIA information can be obtained
at www.ICGtesting.com
Printed in the USA
BVHW071302150419
545535BV00008B/117/P